DICTIONARY

OF

ARBITRATION LAW & PRACTICE

Also by ERIC LEE

Encyclopedia of Arbitration Law (1985)
Commercial Disputes Settlement in China (1985)
Encyclopedia of International Commercial Arbitration (1986)

DICTIONARY

OF

ARBITRATION LAW & PRACTICE

ERIC LEE
BA (Hons), MA(Law), ACIArb.

Mansfield Law Publishers, London
1986

First published - 1986 by
Mansfield Law Publishers, London.
301-305 Euston Road, London NW1 3SS

British Library Cataloguing in Publication Data

Lee, Eric

Dictionary of Arbitration Law & Practice
1. Commercial Law - United Kingdom 2. Arbitration and Award - United Kingdom
I. Title

345.103'7 [Law]

Printed in Great Britain by Robert Hartnoll [1985] Ltd, Cornwall, England.

To

Xuansheng

with love

FOREWORD
by Sir Jack Jacob, Q.C.

This is an admirable work which should prove of great value and importance to all who may be concerned or involved in the machinery of arbitration proceedings. It is much more than a mere "dictionary" in the sense of merely giving the meaning of each word or phrase: it defines, explains and elucidates every chosen term in its legal context and, in particular, in the context of Arbitration Law and Practice. It achieves with great success what appears to be its real objective, which is to throw much light and understanding on the words and phrases in current use among those who are closely involved in arbitration matters. It is a veritable guide and handbook to all the highways and byways of the Arbitration field. It provides a ready reference to a great many points which may not be all that known or familiar. The habit is soon likely to grow for those who are, or may become, involved in arbitration proceedings, to check the relevant entry in this work, just to make sure that they have got it right.

Eric Lee is, therefore, to be congratulated on his imaginative creativity in conceiving and constructing this work. At one stroke, he has fulfilled two important aims at the same time. First, he has filled a very great gap in the literature relating to Arbitration Law and Practice and, secondly, he has supplied a want which must have been felt for a long time. He has performed a great service to the arbitration community, both professionally and non-professionally, and he deserves their great gratitude. For my part, I can warmly commend this work.

PREFACE

Arbitration law and practice in the United Kingdom have undergone rapid changes in recent years. The enactment of the various statutory provisions, the judicial pronouncement of salient points of law when arbitral awards are appealed against and the general increasing awareness of the professional communities of what arbitration can offer, have contributed to dramatic development of arbitration law and practice generally. A welcoming impact of this healthy development is that more and more words and phrases in the arbitration law and practice have their meanings determined and defined by the court and the statutes.

I have endeavoured to collect and select familiar and also less familiar terms in arbitration law and practice, as well as those terms connected therewith, and provide them with definitions or judicial interpretations, with the aim of presenting a readily accessible insight into arbitration law and practice.

This Dictionary, I believe, is the first book of its kind to devote exclusively to arbitration law and practice, and as such, it is hoped that it will be a tool and companion to all those who are interested in, or concerned with, arbitration.

I am greatly indebted to all those who have assisted me in the publication of this book. To Sir Jack, the Director of Institute of Advanced Legal Studies, and formerly Senior Master of the Supreme Court and Queen's Remembrancer, who despite his daily busy schedule and commitments, kindly wrote the Foreword to grace this book; to Laurie Slade, Esq, Legal Adviser and Registrar of the Chartered Institute of Arbitrators, for his indispensable and invaluable assistance; to Victor Lim, Esq, my architect friend, for designing the cover of this book; to John Sinkins, Esq, and Roy Haywood, Esq, both of Wildy and Sons for their brotherly general advice ; and to Roy King, Esq, for his most valued help, I offer my sincere and heartfelt thanks.

The law is stated as at 31 August 1986.

Institute of Advanced Legal Studies
University of London
31 August 1986   ERIC H. K. LEE

Table of Contents

D

E

F

Table of Contents

P

Table of Contents

A

AAA - American Arbitration Association.

ab initio - from the beginning.

abandonment - to give up the whole or part of the claim in an action or an appeal. It is effected in the High Court action when a notice of discontinuance is served. (**See: discontinuance of an action**).

In relation to arbitration, distinction should be drawn from abandonment of a claim or arbitration reference and abandonment of arbitration agreement.

'... the cause of action may survive a consensual termination of the reference. Parties do from time to time agree to end an arbitration: for example, so that they can begin again before another arbitral tribunal or before the High Court. Obviously, in such a case it could not be suggested that the agreement to terminate the reference was *ipso facto* a termination of the claim. Conversely, an express agreement to give up the arbitration might operate, in appropriate circumstances, as an agreement to give up the dispute in all its aspects. In each case, it would be a question of interpreting what the parties said and did.' *Per* Mustill J in *Allied Marine Transport Ltd* v. *Vale do Rio Doce Navegacao SA; The Leonidas D* [1983] 2 Lloyd's Rep 411.

The abandonment of a claim can take place either by accord and satisfaction, or an estoppel. As regards accord and satisfaction, there must be consideration for the abandonment of the claimant's rights: *The Leonidas D* [1983] *(ibid.).*

To enable 'A' to rely on abandonment, he must show that 'B', the opposite party has so conducted himself as to entitle 'A' to assume, and that 'A' does assume, that the contract is agreed to be abandoned: *Cie Francaise d'importation et de Distribution SA* v. *Deutsche Continental Handelsgesellschaft and Another* [1985] 2 Lloyd's Rep 592.

abandonment by both parties, tacit - an arbitration may come to an end by virtue of tacit abandonment by both parties. 'The basis of "tacit abandonment by both parties" ... is that the primary facts are such that it ought to be inferred that the contract to arbitrate the particular dispute was rescinded by the mutual agreement of the parties. To entitle the sellers to rely on abandonment they must show that the buyers so conducted themselves as to entitle the sellers to assume, and that the sellers did assume, that the contract was agreed to be abandoned *sub silentio.' Per* Lord Brightman in *Paal Wilson & Co A/S* v. *Partenreederei Hannah Blumenthal, The Hannah Blumenthal* [1983] 1 Lloyd's Rep 103 at p. 121; [1983] 1 AC 854 at p. 924. **See: abandonment.**

Silence and inactivity of the parties cannot imply consent on the part of the parties to abandonment of the arbitration reference: *Allied Marine Transport Ltd* v. *Vale do Rio Doce Navegacao SA; The Leonidas D* [1985] 2 All ER 796, HL.

"The question whether a contract has been abandoned or not is one of fact." *Per* Lord Brandon of Oakbrook in *The Splendid Sun* [1981] 2 Lloyd's Rep 29 CA at p. 114; [1981] QB 694 at p. 913.

ABTA - Association of British Travel Agents. **See: ABTA arbitration.**

ABTA arbitration - an arbitration scheme administered by the Chartered Institute of Arbitrators on behalf of the Association of British Travel Agents (ABTA) to resolve disputes arising between the tour operators, who are members of the ABTA, and their customers. This arbitration scheme is an optional facility catering for small claims where the amounts involved are less than £1,000 per person or £5,000 per booking form. The scheme is not concerned with disputes about, or arising from, personal injuries or illness. Intending party must claim arbitration within nine months from the date of return from the holiday and agree to be bound by the award. The arbitration is on documents only, without an oral hearing. **See: documentary arbitration.**

abuse of the process of the court - an action in court after an arbitral award has been rendered may be struck out under RSC Order

18, r. 19 on account of an asserted abuse of the process of the court. However, "the allegation that an action is an abuse of the process of the court is a complaint of a procedural rather than a substantive character and the remedy of striking out is likewise a procedural remedy and is always subject to the discretion of the court in deciding whether or not it will grant that procedural remedy. ... the court should consider whether or not it has before it the relevant and necessary information and other material to strike out; if the court considers it has not got the relevant and necessary information and material, the application is prematured; the burden is on the party asserting that there has been an abuse of process to satisfy the court that such is the case; if it is satisfied that there is some good reason for not doing so. If the defendant's assertions that the matter is covered by *res judicata* give rise to triable issues before it can be said that those assertions are to be sustained, then, of course, it follows that those assertions do not alone show that there is an abuse of the process of the court. Litigation which raises triable issues is *prima facie* not an abuse of the court; it is for the determination of such issues that the trial procedure exists." *Per* Hobhouse J in *Dallal* v. *Bank Mellat* [1986] 1 All ER 239 at pp. 247 - 248.

ACAS - Advisory, Conciliation and Arbitration Services.
See: Advisory, Conciliation and Arbitration Services.

accidental slip or omission - unintentional mistake in an award. 'I do not think that it would be right for me to attempt ... to define what is meant by "accidental slip or omission": the animal is, I suspect, usually recognisable when it appears on the scene.': *Per* Robert Goff LJ in *Mutual Shipping Corpn of New York* v. *Bayshore Shipping Co of Monrovia; The Montan* [1985] 1 All ER 520 at p. 529. **See also: slip rule.**

accusatorial procedure - See : **adversary procedure;** contrast: **inquisitorial procedure.**

ACIArb - Associate of the Chartered Institute of Arbitrators.
See: Chartered Institute of Arbitrators.

action - proceeding in a civil court. It is initiated in the High Court by writ, thereby distinguishing it from matters, which are proceedings initiated by other means. **See also:** *in personam; action in rem.*

action *in rem* - an action in the Admiralty Court commenced by the arrest of the *res* , the ship.

action of interdict - term used in Scotland meaning injunction.

actual bias - the attitude of not acting impartially as shown by the arbitrator towards the parties either through his favouritism on one party or on the opposite party; or through his having personal interest on the subject-matter of the dispute. Actual bias need not necessarily be proved if the court when assessed in pursuance of an objective test, is satisfied that 'real likelihood' or 'reasonable suspicion' of bias is present. See the following cases: *R* v. *Moore* [1969] 6 DLR (3d) 465; *Metropolitan Properties Co (FGC) Ltd* v. *Lannon* [1969] 1 QB 577; *Revie* v. *Football Association* (1979) (unreported). *Note:* The judicial argument of whether 'real likelihood' or 'reasonable suspicion' is the correct test is unsettled.
    'With profound respect to those who have propounded the "real likelihood" test, I take the view that the requirement that justice must manifestly be done operates with undiminished force in cases where bias is alleged and that any development of the law which appears to emasculate that requirement should be strongly resisted. That the different tests, even when applied to the same facts, may lead to different results ... But I cannot bring myself to hold that a decision may properly be allowed to stand even although there is *reasonable* suspicion of bias on the part of one or more members of the adjudicating body.' *Per* Edmund Davies LJ in *Metropolitan Properties Co (FGC) Ltd* v. *Lannon* [1969] 1 QB 577 at p. 606.

ad hoc - for this purpose.

ad hoc **arbitration** - an arbitration held between two or more parties, sometimes under certain institutional rules, e.g., the UNCITRAL

Rules, but without the supervision or control of any arbitral body or institution. Thus, an *ad hoc* arbitration is also known as non-institutional arbitration. In Scotland, most arbitrations are *ad hoc* .

adjective or adjectival law - so much of the law as relates to practice and procedure, e.g., law of evidence, law of arbitration.

adjournment - the postponement of the hearing of an action or arbitration reference until a future date. The arbitrator has power to adjourn the hearing so long as the procedure he adopts does not offend the rules of natural justice. Where an arbitrator is asked to adjourn a hearing in order to enable a party to obtain further evidence, he can refuse to accede to the party's application : *The Sanko Steamship Co Ltd* v. *The Shipping Corpn of India and Selwyn and Clark; The Jhansi Ki Rani* [1980] 2 Lloyd's Rep 569; *GKN Centrax Gears Ltd.* v. *Matbro Ltd* [1976] 2 Lloyd's Rep 555.

adjudication - the formal judgment or decision of a court or tribunal.

adjustments - the Scottish equivalent of 'further and better particulars or additions'.

administered arbitration - an arbitration which is held under the control and administration of an institution or a body. For example, Chartered Institute of Arbitrators administers the arbitration where any agreement, submission or reference provides for arbitration under its Rules. All communication between the parties and the arbitrator or arbitrators and between the arbitrator and the parties is to be channelled through the Registrar. The arbitrators are appointed by the Institute and its Rules dictate the exchange of pleadings and other procedures. The Institute charges a fee for the service. **See: Chartered Institute of Arbitrators.**

   In some administered arbitrations, e.g., ICC, the award of the arbitrators is scrutinised and approved by the institution and delivered as the award of the body instead of the arbitrators. **See: ICC arbitration.**

Some administered arbitrations also include a built-in appeal machinery, e.g., GAFTA arbitration, where the award of the arbitrators can be appealed to its Board of Appeal. **See : GAFTA.**

Admiralty Court - that part of the Queen's Bench Division of the High Court, which hears cases concerning ships and the sea. Until 1971, it was part of the Probate, Divorce and Admiralty Division of the High Court. The Admiralty Court may 'arrest' a ship in an *action in rem.* The judge in the Admiralty Court may sit with assessors.

admissibility of evidence - the principle under which the court may receive a particular item of evidence. Relevancy determines admissibility. But where evidence falls within the area of one of the exclusionary rules, evidence that is relevant may be inadmissible. In arbitration references, admissibility of evidence does not necessarily have to follow strict rules of the court unless the parties desired and agreed otherwise. The weight of evidence and the inferences from it are essentially matters for the arbitrator to decide. 'One of the reasons for going to arbitration is to get rid of the technical rules of evidence and so forth'. *Per* Lord Denning in *GKN Centrax Gears Ltd* v. *Matbro Ltd* [1976] 2 Lloyd's Rep 555 at 575.

admission - the statement in a civil proceeding against the other party's case. It may be informed, i.e., contained in a document, or by word of mouth or formal i.e., made in the pleading. It may be made to the court by someone other than the person who made it by virtue of an exception to the rule against hearsay evidence.

adversary procedure - also known as accusatorial procedure. A court procedure in general, adopted by the common-law system, e.g., in England. The characteristic of this procedure is that the judge sits and acts as an impartial umpire and decides the dispute in accordance with evidence submitted and proved before him. He does not lead in the investigations or the examinations of witnesses. Oral hearing and oral examination of witnesses are typical hallmarks of this procedure.

Since English law recognises only the adversary procedure, arbitration held in England is in principle to be conducted under this procedure. Whereas the provision of section 12(1) of the Arbitration Act 1950, relating to the submission of the parties to be examined on oath or affirmation by the arbitrator, may suggest an inquisitorial procedure, regard should be had to Roskill LJ's speech: 'Indeed, an arbitrator or umpire, who in the absence of express agreement that he should do so, attempting to conduct an arbitration along inquisitorial lines might expose himself to criticism and possible removal' : *Bremer Vulkan Schiffbau und Maschinenfabrik* v. *South India Shipping Corpn Ltd* [1981] AC 909 at p. 948. See: **Inquisitorial procedure.**

Advisory, Conciliation and Arbitration Services (ACAS) - This was established by virtue of the Employment Protection Act 1975. Hence, it performs its main function in promoting harmonised industrial relations and the development of collective bargaining through advisory services. So far as arbitration is concerned, ACAS is a misnomer for it does not conduct arbitration in trade disputes. But it may refer a dispute to the Central Arbitration Committee or to an arbitrator, with the consent of the parties. **See : Central Arbitration Committee.**

advocates - persons who present and argue on behalf of litigants in court. Only qualified barristers and solicitors can be advocates. In most Crown Court centres, the High Court, the Court of Appeal and the House of Lords, only barristers can appear as advocates. However, in arbitration reference, the above practice does not apply. A lay man, a technical expert, a barrister or a solicitor or indeed anyone who is of sound mind and of age can appear as an advocate for the parties.

affidavit - sworn written statement to support certain application and, in some cases, used as evidence in court proceedings.

affirmation - (1) the confirmation of the judgment of the lower court by the higher court, or the confirmation of the arbitrator's award by the court on appeal; (2) the alternative form to swearing on oath before giving evidence or when making an affidavit.

The prescribed words of affirmation are: 'I, Smith, do solemnly, sincerely and truly declare and affirm that the evidence I shall give shall be the truth, the whole truth and nothing but the truth'.

Subject to any express provision in the arbitration agreement, the arbitrator has discretion whether or not to examine the witnesses on oath or affirmation: **See:** *Section 12(2), Arbitration Act 1950.*

amiable compositeur - an arbitrator who is authorised and required by the arbitration agreement to decide according to equity and good conscience. **See also: equity,** *ex aequo et bono,* **amiable composition.**

amiable composition - an arbitration where an arbitrator (known as an *amiable compositeur*) is authorised by the arbitration agreement to decide the disputes *ex aequo et bono.* The English law does not authorise such reference. Nevertheless, where a foreign award is obtained under this method, provided it is valid and enforceable in accordance with the *lex fori*, it is enforceable in England. **See:** *amiable compositeur; lex fori; ex aequo et bono.*

ancillary arbitration - the term used in Scotland to describe an arbitration which arises as a result of an agreement to refer future dispute to arbitration, contained in the principal contract dealing with other matters.

This term is also employed in the case where an arbitration is held pursuant to an arbitration agreement to refer future dispute as provided by the rules of an association chosen by the parties.

Anisminic **doctrine** - the principle that an arbitrator must decide in accordance with law. It is named after *Anisminic Ltd* v. *Foreign Compensation Commission* [1969] 2 AC 147.

anticipatory breach - the situation where a party to a contract declares his unwillingness or disability to perform the contract: *Hochester* v. *De la Tour* [1853] 2 E & B 678; *Frost* v. *Knight* (1872) LR 7 Ex 111.

Anton Piller **Order** - an Order named after the case : *Anton Piller KG* v. *Manufacturing Processes* [1976] Ch 55. This Order which is made by the High Court, requires a defendant to permit a plaintiff or his representatives to enter the defendant's premises to inspect or take away material evidence before such evidence is removed or destroyed. The Order is also used to compel a defendant to answer certain questions.

appeal - the examination of the judgment of the lower court by a higher court or the examination of the award of the arbitrator by the court. Under section 18(1)(g) of the Supreme Court Act 1981, no appeal shall lie to the Court of Appeal except as provided by the Arbitration Act 1979, from any decision of the High Court - (i) on any appeal under section 1 of that Act on a question of law arising out of an arbitration award; or (ii) under section 2 of that Act on a question of law arising in the course of a reference. An appeal under section 1 of the Arbitration Act 1979 may be brought by any of the parties to the reference - (a) with the consent of all the other parties to the reference; or (b) subject to section 3 of the Arbitration Act 1979, with the leave of the court: *Section 1(3), Arbitration Act 1979.* An appeal shall lie to the High Court on any question of law arising out of an award made on an arbitration agreement; and on the determination of such an arbitration agreement the High Court may by order - (a) confirm, vary or set aside the award; or (b) remit the award to the reconsideration of the arbitrator or umpire together with the court's opinion on the question of law which was the subject of the appeal: *Section 1(2), Arbitration Act 1979.* In the case of an appeal to the court under section 1(2) of the Arbitration Act 1979, the notice must be served, and the appeal entered, within 21 days after the award has been made and published to the parties. Provided that, where reasons material to the appeal are given on a date subsequent to the publication of the award, the period of 21 days shall run from the date on which the reasons are given ...: *RSC Order 73, r. 5(2).* In the case of every appeal or application to which this rule applies, the notice or originating motion or, as the case may be, the originating summons, must state the grounds of the appeal or application ... *RSC Order 73, r. 5(5).*

'Until 1 October 1983 both the application for leave to appeal and the appeal itself were brought before the court by way of notice of motion and it was the usual practice to incorporate both the application for leave and the notice of motion relating to the appeal in the same document: See:*RSC Order 73, r. 2(2).* Both the application for leave and, if leave were granted, the appeal itself were heard in open court. Since 1 October, however, the application for leave to appeal is brought before the court by summons and is heard in chambers. Some change in the previous practice is therefore necessary.

In future the practice in the ordinary case should be as follows, though there may be exceptional cases where some different course will be more appropriate. A party wishing to appeal should issue an originating notice of motion for the appeal in the Crown Office and should then immediately or shortly thereafter issue an ordinary summons containing the application for leave to appeal in the Commercial Court office. The time limit of 21 days prescribed in Order 73, r. 5(2) should of course be carefully observed: See: Practice Direction issued by Neill J on 18 November 1983, quoted and approved by Bingham J in *Mebro Oil SA* v. *Gatoil International Inc* [1985] 2 Lloyd's Rep 234 at pp. 237-238.

Unless the High Court gives leave, no appeal shall lie to the Court of Appeal from a decision of the High Court - (a) to grant or refuse leave under section 1(3)(b) or section 1(5)(b) of the Arbitration Act 1979; or (b) to make or not to make an order under section 1(5) of the Arbitration Act 1979: *Section 1(6A), Arbitration Act 1979.*

No appeal shall lie to the Court of Appeal unless - (a) the High Court or the Court of Appeal gives leave; and (b) it is certified by the High Court that the question of law to which its decision relates either is one of general public importance or is one which for some other special reason should be considered by the Court of Appeal: *Section 1(7), Arbitration Act 1979.*

Where there is an appeal against an arbitrator's award, it is heard as a separate action from the applications for leave to appeal: *Tor Line AB* v. *Alltrans Group of Canada Ltd* [1982] 1 Lloyd's Rep 617 at pp. 626-627.

See: *Nema* **Guidelines, the; setting aside of award; remission of award; appellate jurisdiction; Commercial Court.**

appellant - a person who makes an appeal to a court or appeals from a lower court to a higher court.

Appellate Committee - see House of Lords.

appellate jurisdiction - the power of a higher court to hear appeals from lower courts or tribunals e.g., the commercial arbitrations, mostly relating to shipping and commodity trading. The Court of Appeal (Civil Division) hears appeals from the County Courts, the High Court in civil cases and also from the Commercial Courts. The House of Lords hears appeals from the Court of Appeal and from the High Court. The House of Lords is also the highest appellate court for Scotland and Northern Ireland.

appointing authority - the authority, which is empowered by the arbitration rules agreed to be adopted by the parties, to appoint arbitrator for the reference. Normally, the authority maintains a panel of arbitrators for this purpose. Some appointing authorities may not act unless and until the parties have failed to act in accordance with the rules. Sometimes, the parties may agree on an independent third person e.g., the president of a learned or professional society, as the appointing authority. Where the Arbitration Act 1950 is applicable to the reference, the court may be approached to act as the appointing authority, if one party fails to appoint his arbitrator: *Section 10(1), Arbitration Act 1950*.

appointment of arbitrator - anyone can be appointed as an arbitrator by the parties if they so agree. The appointment is not normally required to be made by virtue of the appointee's qualification, training, age or status. In spite of the above, certain arbitral associations require that the arbitrator appointed must be a commercial man or someone engaged in the trade.

By virtue of section 1 of the Arbitration Act 1950, the appointment of the arbitrator is irrevocable except by leave of the High Court or a judge thereof. **See also: appointment of arbitrator by implication.**

appointment of arbitrator by implication - the requirement to appoint an arbitrator can be express or implied. Statement by one party that 'I require the difference to be submitted to arbitration in accordance with our agreement' would be sufficient to commence an arbitration, because it would by implication constitute a request to the other to appoint his arbitrator. (See the speech of Lord Denning MR, in *The Agios Lazaros* [1976] 2 Lloyd's Rep 47 at p. 51). A telex from one party to the other claiming arbitration on the disputes which have arisen, constitutes a request, express or implied, to appoint an arbitrator: *Peter Cremer GmbH & Co* v. *Sugat Food Industries Ltd; The Rimon* [1981] 2 Lloyd's Rep 640.

arbiter - the more commonly used term in Scotland meaning arbitrator. The expert in a quality arbitration. **See: quality arbitration.**

arbitrability of the dispute - any dispute in relation to civil law where only damages are claimed may be arbitrable. However, where claims are contrary to public policy, then arbitrability is denied.

Disputes regarding trespass can be arbitrated : *Wrightson* v. *Bywater* (1838) 7 LJ Ex 83. Pure questions of law may be referred to arbitration: *F R Absalom Ltd* v. *Great Western (London) Garden Village Society Ltd* [1933] AC 592. Matters concerning wills may be the subject of an arbitration: *Re Raven* [1915] 1 Ch 673; *Re Wynn* [1952] Ch 271. Even the terms of a separation in matrimonial causes can be arbitrated: *Cahill* v. *Cahill* (1883) 8 App Cas 420 HL.

arbitral tribunal - the tribunal, sometimes known as arbitration court, formed to conduct arbitration reference. It may consist of one arbitrator, in which case, it is known as sole-arbitrator tribunal, (see: **sole arbitrator**) or two arbitrators and an umpire where the umpire only enters upon the reference if and when the two arbitrators disagree: *Termarea SRL* v. *R Sally* [1979] 2 All ER 988 QBD. The sole decision of the umpire is the final award of the tribunal. (**See: umpire**). Sometimes the tribunal is tripartite, and have three arbitrators. In this instance, it is the majority decision of the arbitrators which will constitute the award of the tribunal.

An arbitral tribunal is not an 'inferior court' for the purposes of Order 52, r. 1: *AG* v. *BBC* [1981] AC 303; [1980] 3 All ER 161. The fact that the court may hear an appeal from the arbitral tribunal makes no difference to its status of not being an inferior court: *Shell Co of Australia Ltd* v. *Federal Commissioner of Taxation* [1931] AC 275 at pp. 296-297.

arbitration - a term used to describe a process to settle disputes between two or more parties by referring to one or more persons specially appointed for that purpose, and who are known as arbitrators. It may be a judicial or non-judicial process. The former includes maritime arbitration, legal arbitration etc., which are private arbitrations where disputes are submitted to private tribunals for decision in a judicial manner in accordance with a fixed recognised system of law: *Orion Compania Espanola de Seguros* v. *Belfort Maatschappij Voor Algemene Verzekgringeen* [1962] 2 Lloyd's Rep 257. The decision so delivered shall be final and binding on all parties. The latter comprises industrial arbitration, pay arbitration etc., which are conducted to ascertain the rights and liabilities of the parties. The decisions of the tribunals are merely advisory: See for example, *AG of Australia* v. *R and Boiler Makers' Society of Australia* [1957] AC 288; [1957] 2 All ER 45 PC.

Exercises conducted for valuation, appraisement, or certification are not arbitrations: *Kennedy Ltd* v. *Barrow-in-Furness Corpn* [1909] 2 *Hudson's Building Contracts (4th Edn)* CA; *Northampton Gaslight Co* v. *Parnell* (1855) 15 CB 630; *Sutcliffe* v. *Thackrah and others* [1974] 2 WLR 295 HL.

'An arbitration presupposes the existence of a dispute or disputes between the parties arising out of the contract to which the arbitration clause can apply': *Per* Robert Goff J in *Peter Cremer GmbH & Co* v. *Sugat Food Industries Ltd; The Rimon* [1981] 2 Lloyd's Rep 640 at p. 643.

Arbitration proceedings are not to be assigned to the Chancery Division: *RSC Order 73, r. 1.*

Arbitration Act 1950 - now the principal Act. It came into operation on 1 September 1950: *Section 44(2).* It repealed the Arbitration Act 1889, the Arbitration Clauses (Protocol) Act 1924, the Arbitration (Foreign Awards) Act 1930 and the Arbitration Act 1934. Any reference in any enactment so repealed must be construed as including a reference to the corresponding provision of the Arbitration Act 1950: *Section 44(3), Arbitration Act 1950.*

Part I of the Arbitration Act 1950 (i.e., sections 1-34, general provisions as to arbitration) applies to every arbitration except certain statutory arbitrations where the provisions of the 1950 Act are inconsistent with the relevant statutes: *Section 31(1), Arbitration Act 1950.*

The 1950 Act does not apply to arbitrations held in pursuance of an arbitration agreement which is not in writing: *Section 32, Arbitration Act 1950.*

Arbitration Act 1975 - an Act to give effect to the New York Convention on the Recognition and Enforcement of Foreign Arbitral Awards. The 1975 Act came into operation on 23 December 1975: *SI 1975 No. 1709,* made under section 7(2) of the Arbitration Act 1975. **See: New York Convention.**

Arbitration Act 1979 - an Act to amend the law relating to arbitrations and for the purposes connected therewith. It came into operation as from 1 August 1979: *Section 2, Arbitration Act 1979 (Commencement) Order 1979.* It generally applies to arbitration commenced after 1 August 1979: *Section 2 (ibid.).* But it shall have retroactive effect, if parties, though they may have commenced the reference before the date of coming into force of the Act, agreed in writing that it should apply: *Section 3 (ibid.).*

arbitration agreement - an agreement to refer disputes to arbitration. It can be oral or written. But for Arbitration Act 1950 to apply to the arbitration, it must be in writing. Section 32 of the 1950 Act defines an arbitration agreement as a written agreement to submit present or future differences to arbitration whether an arbitrator is named therein or not.

'For an agreement to be a written agreement to arbitrate it is unnecessary for the whole of the contract, including the arbitration agreement to be contained in the same document. It is sufficient that the arbitration agreement is itself in writing; indeed it is sufficient if there is a document which recognises the existence of an arbitration agreement between the parties.' *Per* Lloyd LJ in *Excomm Ltd* v. *Ahmed Abdul-Qawi Bamaodah; The St Raphael* [1985] 1 Lloyd's Rep 403 at p. 408.

An arbitration agreement can be contained in an exchange of letters or telegrams: *Article II(2), New York Convention, 1958.*

An arbitration agreement which is signed by only one party is a valid arbitration agreement in writing within the meaning of the Arbitration Act 1950: *Metal Traders (UK) Ltd* v. *Sanders Lead International Inc* (1984) 21 March (unreported) (QBD : Lloyd J) See *Halsbury Laws of England (1984) at para 122.*

An arbitration agreement need not be signed: *Excomm Ltd* v. *Ahmed Abdul-Qawi Bamaodah; The St Raphael* [1985]1 Lloyd's Rep 403.

A rent review clause, which does not give bilateral right of reference is not an arbitration agreement within the meaning of the Arbitration Act 1950: *Tote Bookmakers Ltd* v. *Development and Property Holding Co Ltd* [1985] 2 All ER 555.

An agreement to refer disputes to arbitration is subject to the general rules of the law of contract: *Bremer Vulkan Schiffbau und Maschinenfabrik* v. *South India Shipping Corporation Ltd* [1981] 1 Lloyd's Rep 253; [1981] AC 909.

Arbitration agreement can be terminated by mutual consent i.e., when the parties make a further agreement to discharge it: *Paal Wilson & Co A/S* v. *Partenreederei Hannah Blumenthal; The Hannah Blumenthal* [1983] 1 Lloyd's Rep 103 at pp. 114, 115 and 121; [1983] 1 AC 854 HL at pp. 913, 915, 923 and 924. In making the further agreement, the normal rules of law of contract, i.e., rules of offer, acceptance and consideration apply: *Per* Lord Diplock in *The Hannah Blumenthal (Ibid.)* at pp. 115 and 915.

Only if those rules of contract are shown to be complied with that the further agreement to discharge the originating arbitration agreement will have effect: *Allied Marine Transport Ltd* v. *Vale do Rio Doce Navegacao SA; The Leonidas D* [1985] 2 Lloyd's Rep 18; [1985] 1 WLR 925 HL.

Arbitration agreement can bind a third party: *Freshwater* v. *Australian Assurance Co Ltd* [1933] 1 KB 515.

arbitration clause - a term of a contract expressing in writing the intention of the parties to seek recourse through arbitration in the event of disputes arising out of the contract. It is used interchangeably with arbitration agreement. **See also: arbitration agreement; incorporation of arbitration clause.**

arbitration in accordance with strict rules of evidence - normally, arbitration reference need not be conducted under strict rules of evidence. However, where parties agree that an arbitration shall be conducted in accordance with strict rules of evidence, any evidence tendered before the arbitral tribunal is only admissible if the requirements of the Civil Evidence Act 1968 and the rules of court made under it are complied with: *Section 10, Civil Evidence Act 1968*. In this regard, the admissibility of expert evidence is governed by Civil Evidence Act 1972 and the rules of court made under it: *Section 5(2), Civil Evidence Act 1972*.

arbitrator - a person appointed to decide on disputes which have been referred to him for settlement. Depending on the structure of arbitral tribunal, one of the arbitrators in a 3-member tribunal may be an umpire or a presiding chairman. In the case of an umpire, he does not normally have to be appointed unless and until the other two arbitrators disagree:*The Myron* [1969] 1 Lloyd's Rep 411 at p. 415; *Termarea SRL* v. *R Sally* [1979] 2 All ER 988 QBD.

The umpire's sole decision will form the decision of the arbitral tribunal. In the case of a 3-member arbitral tribunal, apart from the chairman having the privilege to rule on certain matter, the award of the tribunal shall be a majority decision.

An architect who issues Certificate to the builders for payment is not an arbitrator: *Sutcliffe* v. *Thackrah and others* [1974] 2 WLR 295 HL. An auditor who determines the values of shares is not an arbitrator: *Arenson* v. *Casson Beckman Rutley & Co* [1977] AC 405 HL. A conciliator is not an arbitrator: *Charles* v. *Cardiff Collieries Ltd* (1928) 44 TLR 448 CA. A valuer is not an arbitrator: *Taylor* v. *Yielding* (1912) 56 Sol Jo 253; *Palacath Ltd* v. *Flanagan* [1985] 2 All ER 161.

An arbitrator is neither more nor less than a private judge of a private court (called an arbitral tribunal) who gives a private judgment (called an award): *Russell on Arbitration.*

arbitrator's fee - the arbitrator may charge a fee for his services rendered in the arbitration reference. Where the arbitration is institutional or administered, the arbitrator will charge a fee in accordance with the scale of fees fixed by the institution concerned. Some institutions fix the arbitrator's fee in relation to the number of hours or days of services rendered, e.g., the fees may be £350 per hour, while others fix the scale of fee according to the amount of the dispute involved e.g., 0.5% of the amount in dispute. (see: **institutional arbitration; administered arbitration**). In an *ad hoc* arbitration, the arbitrator fixes his own fee and his charges are liable to taxation. Excessive fee charged by the arbitrator may be misconduct: *re An Arbitration between Prebble and Robinson and another* [1892] 2 QB 602. But what is excessive charge or extravagant fee depends on the standing of the arbitrator: *Appleton* v. *Norwich Union Fire Insurance Society Ltd* (1922) 13 Ll LR 345. It is doubtful whether an arbitrator can sue for his fee in the absence of express or implied agreement to remunerate him for his service. But the arbitrator has a lien on the award and the documents until his fees are paid: *Roberts* v. *Eberhardt* (1857) 3 CB NS 482; 28 LJ CP 74; 32 LT OS 36. However, under section 19(1) of the Arbitration Act 1950, if an arbitrator or umpire refuses to deliver up his award except on payment of his fees, on the application of one of the parties, the Court may order him to deliver the award subject to the applicant paying the demanded arbitrator's fee into court. The fees shall then be taxed by the taxing office. Any excessive charge will then be refunded to the parties. Section 19(1) does not apply in the case where the fees have been fixed by written agreement between the arbitrator and the parties: *Section 19(2), Arbitration Act 1950.*

arbitrator's jurisdiction - the arbitrator derives his jurisdiction to conduct the reference and to decide the dispute from the arbitration agreement.

Where arbitrator's jurisdiction is in doubt, he cannot decide his own jurisdiction: *Heyman* v. *Darwins* (1942) 72 Ll LR 65.

'Therefore, whenever a question arises whether or not there has been a submission to arbitration, an arbitrator cannot in English law decide that issue. The only tribunal to decide it is the court ...' *Per* Roskill LJ in *Willcock* v. *Pickfords Removal Ltd* [1979] 1 Lloyd's Rep 244 CA.

Atlantic Shipping Clause - a form of arbitration clause which provides that any claim to which it applies shall be barred unless arbitration proceedings are commenced within a certain time-limit as opposed to the time-limit provided under the Limitation Act 1980. The clause takes its name from *Atlantic Shipping & Trading Co* v. *Louis Dreyfus Co* [1922] All ER Rep 559. An example of the clause: 'A party claiming arbitration (otherwise than in respect of condition and/or quality) must appoint his arbitrator and must make his claim for arbitration and give notice of appointment of his arbitrator in writing to the other party within six calender months of the expiry of the contract time of shipment or of the date of completion of final discharge of the ship at port of destination under this contract, whichever period shall last expire': *Panchaud Freres SA* v. *Etablissements General Grains Co* [1970] 1 Lloyd's Rep 53.

The objects of such a clause are: (a) to provide some limit to the uncertainties and expenses of arbitration and litigation; (b) to facilitate the obtaining of material evidence (*per* Mocatta J in *The Himmerland* [1965] 2 Lloyd's Rep 353 at p. 360); and (c) to facilitate the settling of accounts for each voyage as and when they fall due (*per* Lord Denning MR in *Agro Co of Canada Ltd* v. *Richmond Shipping Ltd; The Simonburn* [1973] 1 Lloyd's Rep 392 at p. 394.)

The court has power, under section 27 of the Arbitration Act 1950, to extend the time-limit, if it is of opinion that in the circumstances of the case undue hardship would otherwise be caused, and on such terms as the justice of the case may require. **See: extension of time.**

autonomy of the arbitration clause - the principle that an arbitration clause is independent of the main or principal contract which contains the arbitration clause. This principle has now been approved in English law by virtue of Lord Diplock's speech in *Bremer Vulkan Schiffbau und Maschinenfabrik* v. *South India Shipping Corpn* [1981] 2 WLR 141 HL; [1981] 1 All ER 289; [1980] 1 Lloyd's Rep 255.

award - decision or judgment of the arbitrator after a judicial exercise of considering all evidence and arguments tendered before him by the parties, including examination and cross-examination (if any) of such evidence. The award is final and binding between the parties. It can be interim or final. However, for the purposes of Part II of the Arbitration Act 1950, relating to enforcement of certain foreign awards, an award shall not be deemed final if any proceeding for the purpose of contesting the validity of the award are pending in the country in which it was made. **See: interim award; final award.**

For the purpose of the New York Convention 1958, arbitral awards shall include not only awards made by arbitrators appointed for each case but also those made by permanent arbitral bodies to which the parties have submitted (such as the ICC): *Article I(2), New York Convention 1958*. **See also: ICC arbitration.**

Where the Arbitration Act 1979 applies, an award must contain reasons so that if there is an appeal, it will enable the court to consider any question of law arising out of the award: *Section 1(5), Arbitration Act 1979*. **See: reasoned award.**

An award on an arbitration agreement may, by leave of the High Court or a judge thereof, be enforced in the same manner as a judgment or order to the same effect: *Section 26(1), Arbitration Act 1950*.

In all cases of reference to arbitration, the High Court or a judge thereof may from time to time remit the matters referred, or any of them to the reconsideration of the arbitrator or umpire: *Section 22(1), Arbitration Act 1950*. **See: remission of award; appeal.**

Where an arbitrator or umpire has misconducted himself or the proceedings, or an arbitration or award has been improperly procured, the High Court may set the award aside: *Section 23(2), Arbitration Act 1950*. **See: misconduct; setting aside of award; remission of award.**

All right to set aside or remit an award for error of fact or law on its face has been abolished by section 1 of the Arbitration Act 1979 and substituted with a limited right of appeal on questions of law, based on the arbitrator's reasons for his award.

An award must be signed by the arbitrator. But it need not be signed by all the arbitrators at the same time and place, though in some arbitral rules e.g., the ICC, this must be so: *European Grain & Shipping Ltd.* v. *Johnston* [1982] 3 All ER 989 CA. However, to sign an award without participating in the arbitration reference is misconduct by the arbitrator and this will result in the award to be set aside: *European Grain & Shipping Ltd* v. *Johnston* [1982] 3 All ER 989 CA.

Apart from monetary award, an arbitrator has power to order specific performance, in the absence of contrary intention of the parties: *Section 15 of the Arbitration Act 1950.* **See: specific performance.** A failure to honour an award gives rise to an independent cause of action: *Agromet Motoimport Ltd* v. *Maulden Engineering Co (Beds) Ltd* [1985] 2 All ER 436.

B

bailiff - one of the officers of the court (usually a county court) whose duties include the services of court's processes and the enforcement of its orders, especially warrants of execution authorising the seizure of the goods of debtors.

bailiwick - the area within which a bailiff exercises jurisdiction.

'Baltime 1939' charterparty arbitration clause - "any dispute arising under this Charter to be referred to arbitration in London (or such other place as may be agreed [in Box 24]), one Arbitrator to be nominated by the owners and the other by the Charterers, and in case the Arbitrators shall not agree then to the decision of an Umpire to be appointed by them, the award of the Arbitrators or the Umpire to be final and binding upon both parties": *Clause 23, Baltime Form.*

BIAC - British Institute of Agricultural Consultants. **See: British Institute of Agricultural Consultants.**

bias - the state of mind of an arbitrator who acts partially in a reference. It may arise under two different contexts: as between the arbitrator and one of the disputant parties; and as between the arbitrator and the subject-matter of the dispute. General principles of law apply in relation to bias of the arbitrator. Moreover, an arbitrator would be removed for having misconducted himself if found guilty of bias, under section 23(2), Arbitration Act 1950. The appointment of the arbitrator may also be revoked if he is found guilty of not acting impartially, under section 24(1), Arbitration Act 1950. See the case of *re An Arbitration between the owners of steamship Catalina and others and the owners of motor vessel Norma* (1938) 61 Ll LR 360. **See also: actual bias; imputed bias.**

bilateral discharge - the mutual agreement to end a contract before neither party has yet performed his obligations under the contract. **Compare: unilateral discharge.**

Bill of Lading - a document signed by the carrier and issued to the shipper, in carriage of goods. It constitutes (a) evidence of the contract; (b) a receipt for the goods shipped; and (c) a document of title. It usually contains, *inter alia,* an arbitration clause.

Under the Bills of Lading Act 1855, every consignee of goods named in a bill of lading, and every indorsee of a bill of lading to whom the property in the goods passed on or by reason of such consignment or indorsement, shall have transferred to him all rights of suit, and be subject to the same liabilities as if the contract contained in the bill of lading had been made with himself: *Section 1;* (ii) nothing in the Act shall prejudice any right of stoppage in transit or any right to claim freight against the original shipper or owner: *Section 2*; and (iii) every bill of lading in the hands of a consignee or indorsee for valuable consideration, representing goods to have been shipped on board a vessel, is conclusive evidence of such shipment as against the master or other person signing the bill of lading, notwithstanding that such goods or some part of them may not have been shipped unless the holder of the bill of lading had actual notice at the time of receiving the goods that they had, in fact, been loaded: *Section 3*. See also: **incorporation of arbitration clause.**

BLGIA - British Liaison Group for International Arbitrations. **See: British Liaison Group for International Arbitrations.**

Books of Council and Session - one of the official registers of the Scottish Courts. Certain decree-arbitral can be registered in these records. **See also: decree-arbitral.**

British Institute of Agricultural Consultants - a professional body which advises on litigations and arbitrations relating to agricultural trade. Many of the more senior members of the Institute have been involved in acting as expert witnesses in the court. The Institute also provides a dispute resolution service known as Arbitration, Adjudication and Conciliation Service. The arbitrations mainly concern rent reviews, notice to quit and other claims arising from the Agricultural Holding Act 1948; and also those arbitrations concerning the Dairy Produce Quotas Regulations 1984, i.e., the Milk Quota Arbitrations. *Note*: with effect from 18 June 1986, the appointments of arbitrators for the arbitrations under the Agricultural Holding Act 1948 are no longer made by the Minister of Agriculture, but by the President of the Royal Institutions of Chartered Surveyors (RICS). See section 12(3)(b), Agricultural Holding Act 1986. **See also: statutory arbitrations.**

British law - English law in a London arbitration clause: *Laertis Shipping Corpn* v. *Exportadora Espanola de Cementos Portland SA; The Laertis* [1982] 1 Lloyd' s Rep 613.

British Liaison Group for International Arbitrations - an umbrella organisation which exists to promote and support international arbitration in the United Kingdom. The BLGIA has no secretariat of its own but it functions through the Chartered Institute of Arbitrators. Its membership consists of thirty-five professional and trade organisations which are involved in international arbitrations.

British Telecom arbitration - an arbitration service offered by the Chartered Institute of Arbitrators for the British Telecom customers relating to claims arising out of its services covered in its Code of Practice for Consumers. Disputes involving sums not greater than £1,000 and not involving a complicated issue of law are admissible under this procedure: *Rule 1.2 Chartered Institute of Arbitrators - British Telecommunications plc Arbitration Rules, (October 1984 Edition - Interim Procedure.)*

A consumer must claim arbitration within 12 months from the date on which he or she receives the last reply from the British Telecom. Once claimed, the consumer will be precluded from commencing legal action in court: *Rule 1.4 and Rule 1.7, Ibid.*

The arbitration will be on documents only and the award is final and binding on the parties, subject to the right of appeal to the court within the ambit of the Arbitration Acts 1950-1979: *Rule 3.1, Rule 5.4 and Rule 5.5, Ibid.*

C

CA - Court of Appeal. **See: Court of Appeal.**

Carriage of Goods by Sea Act 1924 - see: **Hague Rules.**

Carriage of Goods by Sea Act 1971 - an enabling Act to bring the Hague-Visby Rules into force. **See: Hague-Visby Rules.**

case - (1) a legal dispute; (2) a court action; (3) an arbitration reference; and (4) the arguments collectively, put forward by either side in an arbitration reference or action in court.

case law - the body of law arising from judicial decision of the court. Arbitral awards, *per se*, do not form part of the case law as the awards have no binding effects apart from on the parties concerned. **See: precedents.**

case stated - a written statement submitted to the High Court for its opinion on any question of law. An aggrieved party to the proceeding by the decisions can request the court to state a case. Section 21 of the Arbitration Act 1950 (repealed by section 8(3)(b) of the Arbitration Act 1979, save where arbitration has been commenced before 1 August 1979 and where the parties have not agreed in writing that the Arbitration Act 1979 is to apply in the arbitration) provides:
 (1) an arbitrator or umpire may, and shall if so directed by the High Court, state (a) any question of law arising in the court of the reference; or (b) an award or any part of an award in the form of a special case for the decision of the High Court;
 (2) a special case with respect to an interim award or with respect to a question of law arising in the course of a reference may be stated, or may be directed by the High Court to be stated, notwithstanding that proceedings under the reference are still pending.
 (3) a decision of the High Court under this section shall be deemed to be a judgment of the court within the meaning of section

twenty-seven of the Supreme Court of Judicature (Consolidation) Act 1925 (which relates to the jurisdiction of the Court of Appeal to hear and determine appeals from any judgment of the High Court), but no appeal shall lie from the decision of the High Court on any case stated under paragraph (a) of subsection (1) of this section without the leave of the High Court or of the Court of Appeal.

See also: special case procedure.

cause - a court action.

Cause Book - the book recording the issue of writs in the Central Office of the Supreme Court and certain later stages of the court proceedings.

Cause List - a list of cases displayed in the court providing information as to when a case will be heard. It appears in the form of the *Daily Cause List* and contains the *warned list* of cases about to be listed for hearing.

cause of action - the grounds that entitle a person to bring an action. It may be a wrongful act or harm resulting from a wrongful act, as in the case of negligence.

Central Arbitration Committee - a body established under the Employment Protection Act 1975, to determine disputes relating to (a) arbitration in trade disputes referred to it by ACAS with the agreement of the parties; (b) disclosure of information to trade unions; (c) the Fair Wages Resolution 1946; (d) the application of the Equal Pay Act 1970; and (e) statutory requirements concerning pay and conditions of employment in the road transport, film and independent broadcasting industries.

The Chairman and the Committee members are appointed by the Secretary of State for Employment from persons nominated by ACAS.

The award of pay and/or conditions of employment of the Committee are generally incorporated in an individual employee's contract of employment. These awards are not, *per se*, legally binding and as such, parties would have to seek enforcement in the courts.

Moreover, the awards are enforceable in the courts only if the parties have agreed before the commencement of the arbitration that they would accept the awards rendered as binding. Thus, it is the usual practice for ACAS to insist on such undertaking of the parties before an arbitration is set up. **See also: ACAS.**

Centrocon arbitration clause - 'all disputes from time to time arising out of the contract shall, unless the parties agree forthwith on a single Arbitrator, be referred to the final arbitrament of two Arbitrators carrying on business in London who shall be Members of the Baltic and engaged in the Shipping and/or Grain trades, one to be appointed by each of the parties, with power to such Arbitrators to appoint an Umpire. Any claim must be made in writing and Claimant's Arbitrator appointed within three months of final discharge and where this provision is not complied with the claims shall be deemed to be waived and absolutely barred. No award shall be questioned or invalidated on the ground that any of the Arbitrators is not qualified as above, unless objection to his acting be taken before the award is made.'

Ch - Chancery Division. **See Chancery Division.**

Chancery Division - that part of the High Court of Justice created by the Judicature Acts 1873-75 replacing the then Court of Chancery. The jurisdiction of the Chancery Division includes matters relating to real property, trusts, company law, patent, etc. Arbitration proceedings are not to be assigned to the Chancery Division: *RSC Order 73, r. 1.*
    Although the Lord President is the designated head of the Division, in practice, its head is the Vice Chancellor.

charter - (1) a document evidencing something done between one party and another. **See: charterparty**; (2) the grant of rights and privileges by the Crown e.g., a royal charter to a university or an institution. The Chartered Institute of Arbitrators received its Royal Charter in 1979.

Chartered Institute of Arbitrators, the (CIArb) - founded in 1915, the Institute is one of the oldest and largest arbitral organisations in the world. In 1979, it received its Royal Charter. Today, it has a membership of more than 6,000 from all over the world, although the majority of them are from the United Kingdom.

The Institute provides training to its members and also members of other professional bodies in furtherance of the cause of arbitration. Apart from administering arbitrations conducted under its rules, the Institute also supports other organisations to administer arbitrations on their behalf, e.g., ABTA arbitration. In this regard, it publishes rules for arbitration in general and for small claims consumer arbitrations, e.g., Post Office arbitration, and maintains panels of arbitrators. **See also: consumer arbitration.**

The CIArb also jointly manages the London Court of International Arbitration with the Corporation of the City of London and the London Chamber of Commerce and Industry.

charterparty - a contract of hire of either an entire ship or some principal part of it. Thus, a *time charter* (or charterparty) is the contract of hire for a specific period and that of the *voyage charter* (or charterparty) for a specific voyage or voyages. There is a third type of charterparty - *charter by demise.* This gives the charterers full possession and control of the ship, i.e., the charterers put their own stores, fuel, oil, etc., on board and hire their own crew.

Some terms in the charterparty are construed as conditions while others are warranties. There are a number of standard charterparty forms used commonly in the trade and they usually contain an arbitration clause.

CIArb - the Chartered Institute of Arbitrators. **See: Chartered Institute of Arbitrators, the.**

CIArb arbitration clause - 'any dispute or difference of any kind whatsoever which arises or occurs between the parties in relation to any thing or matter arising under, out of, or in connection with this agreement shall be referred to arbitration under the Arbitration Rules of the Chartered Institute of Arbitrators.'

circuit judge - a judge who normally sits in the County Court or a Crown Court. He is appointed under the provisions of the Courts Act 1971 from among barristers of not less than 10 years' standing or solicitors who have been recorders for at least three years. He may also sit in the High Court, if by invitation of the Lord Chancellor.

Circuit judge in the County Court is prohibited from sitting as private arbitrator for a fee to himself: *Section 6(b), County Courts Act 1956.*

citation - Scots equivalent of subpoena.

Civil Court - a court which hears civil cases. In England, the civil courts are County Courts, High Court and the Court of Appeal (Civil Division). The Appellate Committee of the House of Lords hears both civil and criminal appeal.

Civil law - (1) Roman law; (2) the law of a State, sometimes known as municipal law, domestic law or national law; (3) a system of law based on Roman law; thus the civil law system practised mainly by the European continental countries; (4) private law e.g., law of contract, trust, etc., as opposed to criminal law, administrative law, military law and ecclesiastical law.

civil proceedings - actions in court seeking for civil remedies such as damages, injunction, etc. For the purposes of the Civil Evidence Act 1968, civil proceedings include, in addition to civil proceedings in any of the ordinary courts of law:- (a) civil proceedings before any other tribunal, being proceedings in relation to which the strict rules of evidence apply; and (b) an arbitration or reference, whether under an enactment or not, but does not include civil proceedings in relation to which the strict rules of evidence do not apply: *Section 18(1), Civil Evidence Act 1968.*

claim - (1) a demand for a remedy or assertion of right; (2) in proceedings, the claim is known as Statement of Claim; (3) in arbitration, a party claims arbitration in pursuance of the arbitration agreement or clause.

What amounts to a 'claim', in section 27 of the Arbitration Act 1950, see: *Sioux Inc* v. *China Salvage Co, Kwangchow Branch and another; The American Sioux* [1980] 3 All ER 154 at pp. 158-159.

claimant - the party who initiates the arbitration reference. Compare: plaintiff in an action in court. **See also: plaintiff.**

claused reasons - restricted reasons which are provided with the award and have the condition that they can only be used in connection with the award. As a matter of contract, where an award contains claused reasons, the parties have agreed with each other and the arbitrator to treat such reasons as confidential and claused. This, as a matter of contract, precludes any party, except by agreement, from referring to them on any application to the court. The contract which imposes and accepts the obligation of confidence is one which comes into existence either when the parties concur in asking the arbitrator for such reasons or, when an arbitrator where there has been no request for reasons, supplies the parties with restricted reasons and the parties accept such reasons from the arbitrator: See the speech of Hobhouse J in *Mutual Shipping Corpn of New York* v. *Bayshore Shipping Co of Monrovia; The Montan* [1985] 1 All ER 520 CA at p. 523.

'Where restricted reasons are given and accepted by the parties, the parties must be deemed to have agreed that the reasons cannot be placed before the court, such an agreement purports to oust the jurisdiction of the court and is void as having contrary to public policy ... were it otherwise the court would be powerless in the face of misconduct or even fraud revealed by the restricted reasons. We can therefore look at [the arbitrator's] reasons.' *Per* Sir John Donaldson MR in *Mutual Shipping Corpn of New York* v. *Bayshore Shipping Co of Monrovia; The Montan* [1985] 1 All ER 520 CA at p. 523.

'Whichever way of looking ... it is clear to my mind that the parties themselves cannot blindfold the court [by virtue of restricted or claused reasons], only the court itself can do that and on the vast majority of cases it will do so.' *Per* Sir Roger Ormrod in *Mutual Shipping Corpn of New York* v. *Bayshore Shipping Corpn of Monrovia; The Montan (ibid.)* at p. 523.

'Few nations are prepared to lead the power of the state to enforcing arbitration awards without retaining some right to review the awards themselves. This is reflected in the New York Convention ... which has been incorporated into English domestic law by the Arbitration Act 1975. Section 5 of that Act sets out circumstances which would justify the courts of the convention country in refusing to enforce an award. The reasons for an award can certainly be referred to in order to demonstrate that such circumstances exist.' *Per* Sir John Donaldson MR in *Mutual Shipping Corpn of New York* v. *Bayshore Shipping Co of Montovia; The Montan (ibid.)* at p. 523.

clerk - a solicitor appointed by an arbiter in Scotland to provide - (1) secretarial or administrative services required for the proceedings; and (2) the arbiter with legal advice. This practice of appointing a solicitor as an arbiter's clerk is a common one, unless the arbiter himself is a lawyer and the amount in dispute is small.

close of pleading - in an action in the High Court, the close of pleading is 14 days after service of the reply or, if there is no reply but only a defence to counterclaim, 14 days after service of the defence to counterclaim. The stage of close of pleading is important since it fixes the date by reference to which the summons for directions must be issued and it creates an implied joinder of issue on the pleading last served.

In an arbitration reference, the close of pleading is usually determined by the arbitrator who normally follow the practice in court, during the preliminary meeting, unless otherwise agreed by the parties.

commencement of arbitration under Arbitration Act 1950 - section 29(2) of the 1950 Act provides:- '... an arbitration shall be deemd to be commenced when one party to the arbitration agreement serves on the other party or parties a notice requiring him or them to appoint or concur in appointing an arbitrator, or, where the arbitration agreement provides that the reference shall be to a person named or designated in the agreement, requiring him or them to submit the dispute to the person so named or designated.'.

'In order to commence the arbitration, there must, I think, be a notice in writing served by one party on the other party. This notice must contain a requirement. It must require the other party to do one or other of two things: (1) Either "to appoint an arbitrator"; or (2) to agree to the appointment of an arbitrator ...

The first alternative (1) is appropriate in a case where the reference is to two arbitrators, one to be appointed by each party. In such a case the arbitration is deemed to commence when the one party, expressly or by implication, requires the other party to appoint his arbitrator. If he simply says: "I require the difference to be submitted to arbitration in accordance with our agreement" that is sufficient to commence the arbitration: because it is by implication a request to the other to appoint his arbitrator." ' *Per* Lord Denning in *The Agios Lazaros* [1976] 2 Lloyd's Rep 47 at p. 51.

commencement of arbitration under Arbitration Act 1975 - if any party to an arbitration agreement to which this section applies commences any legal proceedings ... (*section 1(1) of the 1975 Act*). 'Ought that word [i.e., commences] to be read as relating only to commencement of proceedings by a person who is then party to the relevant arbitration proceedings? Or ought it to be read as referring to commencement at any time, including commencement before the arbitration agreement has been made? An absolutely literal construction favours the first approach, but regard to the purpose of the sub-section would appear to favour the second approach, because it is not apparent why the Court's duty to stay proceedings should not equally apply where an arbitration has been entered into after proceedings have been commenced. I am inclined to prefer the latter approach. There is however here an ambiguity, and since the Act was passed to give effect to the New York Convention on the Recognition and Enforcement of Foreign Arbitration Awards, it is legitimate in such circumstances to have regard to the treaty: See: *The Eschersheim,* [1976] 2 Lloyd's Rep 1 HL; [1976] 1 WLR. 430; [1976] 1 All ER 920.

... Recourse to the treaty therefore favours the second approach, which I myself have been inclined to accept as a matter of construction. In the circumstances, I would reject the literal approach, ...' *Per* Robert Goff LJ in *The Tuyuti* [1984] 2 All ER 545 at p. 555.

commencement of arbitration under Limitation Act 1980 - Section 34 : '(3) For the purposes of this Act and of any other limitation enactment an arbitration shall be treated as being commenced - (a) when one party to the arbitration serves on the other party or parties a notice requiring him or them to appoint an arbitrator or to agree to the appointment of an arbitrator; or (b) where the arbitration agreement provides that the reference shall be to a person named or designated in the agreement, when one party to the arbitration serves on the other party or parties a notice requiring him or them to submit the dispute to the person so named or designated; (4) Any such notice may be served either - (a) by delivering it to the person on whom it is to be served; or (b) by leaving it at the usual or last-known place of abode in England and Wales of that person; or (c) by sending it by post in a registered letter addressed to that person at his usual or last-known place of abode in England and Wales; as well as in any other manner provided in the arbitration agreement. (5) ... (6) This section shall apply to an arbitration under an Act of Parliament as well as to an arbitration pursuant to an arbitration agreement.

Subsections (3) and (4) above, shall have effect, in relation to an arbitration under an Act, as if for the references to the arbitration agreement there were substituted references to such of the provisions of the Act or of any order, scheme, rules, regulations or byelaws made under the Act as relate to the arbitration.'

commercial action - any cause arising out of the ordinary transactions of merchants and traders and, without prejudice to the generality of the foregoing words, any cause relating to the construction of a mercantile document, the export or import of merchandise, affreightment, insurance, banking, mercantile agency and mercantile usage: *RSC Order 72, r . 1(2)*.

commercial causes - court actions arising out of transactions among merchants and traders. **See also: commercial action.**

Commercial Court - the Commercial Court came into existence in 1970 by virtue of section 3 of the Administration of Justice Act 1970, to take such causes and matters as may in accordance with rules of Court be entered in the Commercial List.

Section 3 above has been repealed and superseded by the Supreme Court Act 1981. Section 6 of the 1981 Act provides: '(1) There shall be - (a) ... (b) as parts of the Queen's Bench Division, an Admiralty Court and a Commercial Court; (2) The judges of the Admiralty Court and of the Commercial Court shall be such of the puisne judges of the High Court as the Lord Chancellor may from time to time nominate to be ... Admiralty Judges and Commercial Judges respectively.'

By virtue of the introduction of RSC Order 73, r. 6 in 1979, all applications arising out of any arbitration which under sections 2 and 3 of the Arbitration Act 1979 have to be heard by a judge, usually have to come before a commercial judge. The applications under the Arbitration Acts 1950-1979 to the Commercial Court are as follows:

Under the 1950 Act : (a) to remit an award under section 22; (b) to remove an arbitrator or umpire under section 23(1); and (c) to set aside an award under section 23(2).

Under the 1979 Act : (a) for leave to appeal under section 2(1); (b) for determination of any question of law under section 2(1); and (c) for an order requiring an arbitrator or umpire to give reasons for his awards under section 1(5); (d) for an order to enhance the power of an arbitrator under section 5.

commercial judges - those puisne judges of the Queen's Bench Division nominated by the Lord Chancellor, to sit in the Commercial Court by virtue of their special experience of commercial matters. **See: puisne judge; Commercial Court.**

commercial list - a list of cases arising out of transactions among merchants and traders assigned to be tried and heard by the Queen's Bench Division, and now particularly, the Commercial Court of the Queen's Bench Division. **See also: commercial action; Commercial Court.**

commercial man - the rules of some arbitral institutions, e.g., GAFTA, require that the person appointed as an arbitrator must be a commercial man. A lawyer cannot be a commercial man: *Rahcassi Shipping Co SA* v. *Blue Star Line Ltd* [1967] 3 All ER 301. But a person who is actively engaged throughout all available working hours in maritime arbitrations is regarded in practice as being engaged in the shipping trade: *The Myron (Owner)* v. *Tradax Export SA* [1969] 1 Lloyd's Rep 411. A full-time maritime arbitrator is considered to be a commercial man: *Pando Compania Naviera SA* v. *Filmo SAS* [1975] 1 Lloyd's Rep 560.

commodity contract - a contract for the sales of goods regularly dealt with on a commodity market or exchange in England or Wales which is specified for the purposes of section 4 of the Arbitration Act 1979 by an order made by the Secretary of State. This Order which is cited as the Arbitration (Commodity Contracts) Order 1979 came into operation on 1 August 1979: *SI 1979 No. 754.*

Common law - that part of English law developed by the royal courts through their judgments over the years as the result of the principle of *stare decisis.* **See: precedent;** *stare decisis.*

compensation - monetary payment for loss or damage.

competence (of witnesses) - the legal capacity of a person to be a witness.

complaint - the initiating step in civil proceeding consisting of a statement of the complainant's allegations.

compromise - the settlement of a dispute by agreement between the parties, even when proceedings are in progress. In such an event, all proceedings are to be terminated. In court proceeding, the terms of the settlement may be incorporated in the judgment, known as the consent judgment. In arbitration, the arbitrator may proceed to give his award based on the terms agreed, and the award is known as the consent award. **See: consent award.**

compromissarii sunt judices - arbitrators are judges (Latin).

conciliation - a method of resolving disputes by negotiation either between the parties or through the intervention of an independent third body. **See: conciliators.** Both the UNCITRAL and the ICC have Conciliation Rules to assist parties resorting to this procedure.

The main characteristic of conciliation is that: it can begin or terminate according to the wish of the parties and can be less formal in procedures than arbitration.

The settlement reached at a conciliation is not an arbitration award and as such can only be enforced as a contract in a subsequent arbitration or judicial proceeding. **See: conciliatory statement.**

Conciliation has not been recognised in English law as a formal institution. Most conciliations are conducted by solicitors alongside actions in court or arbitration upon 'without prejudice' procedure. About 80 to 90 per cent of cases are settled through solicitors' conciliation under the name of 'without prejudice' discussions.

conciliators - persons called upon to conduct conciliation with a view to resolving disputes between two parties. In performing their functions, they are generally required to follow the principles of fairness and justice and give due regard to legal rights and obligations of parties as well as applicable trade usages.

The chairman of a conciliation board is not an arbitrator: *Charles v. Cardiff Collieries Ltd* (1928) 44 TLR 448 CA; *Cardiff Collieries Ltd v. Meredith* (1928) 45 TLR 321 HL.

conciliatory statement - the decision and recommendation of the conciliator for the purpose of voluntary enforcement by the parties. It may be a statement of fact for any subsequent arbitration or actions in court.

concurrent hearing - the hearing of two or more cases simultaneously by the same tribunal. An arbitrator has no power to order concurrent hearing of two arbitrations without the consent of the parties: *Oxford Shipping Co* v. *Nippon Yusen Kaisha; The Eastern Saga* [1984] 2 Lloyd's Rep 373; [1984] 3 All ER 835.

condition - in contract, it is a major term which is also the essence of the contract. The breach of it goes to the root of the contract. It may be express or implied.

condition precedent - a provision which does not form part of a contractual obligation but operates to suspend the contract upon the happening of a certain event, e.g., where 'A' agrees to resort to arbitration before bringing an action in court. **See:** *Scott* v. *Avery Clause*; also: **condition subsequent.**

condition subsequent - a contractual term that brings the contract to an end upon specified circumstances, e.g., the term in a contract of sale specifying the right of a buyer to return the goods purchased within 14 days. **See also: condition precedent.**

confidential reasons - a misnomer for claused or restricted reasons since these reasons can be looked at and the only restriction is on using them in connection with the award. See the speech of Sir John Donaldson MR in *Mutual Shipping Corpn of New York* v. *Bayshore Shipping Co of Monrovia; The Montan* [1985] 1 All ER CA 520 at p. 523. **See: claused reasons.**

conflict of laws : see private international law.

consent award - the award rendered as the result of a negotiated settlement between the parties at the interlocutory stage or during the hearing. The arbitrator will set out the terms of the settlement and incorporate them in his award. Such an award is enforceable in the same manner as any other award, under section 26 of the Arbitration Act 1950. Contrast: **conciliatory statement.**

consolidation of actions - the trial of two or more actions together in a civil action, with the view to saving costs and time. Some common questions of law or facts must be shown to exist before a consolidation can be ordered.

However, in arbitration, no consolidation of references is possible, since arbitration is basically a private procedure. (**See:**

private arbitration). Unless with the consent of the parties, a dispute cannot be heard with another dispute under a different arbitration agreement, although these two disputes are closely related and such consolidation of actions is mutually convenient: *Oxford Shipping Co Ltd* v. *Nippon Yusen Kaisha; The Eastern Saga* [1984] 2 Lloyd's Rep 373; [1984] 3 All ER 835. '... English arbitration law provides at present no power either to arbitrators or the Court to ensure that both arbitrations will be considered by the same tribunal either at the same hearing or at immediately succeeding hearings to avoid the danger of inconsistent awards. There is, for example, no means of ordering consolidation of two such related arbitrations.' *Per* Robert Goff LJ in *Interbulk Ltd* v. *Aiden Shipping Co Ltd; ICCO International Corn Co NV* v. *Interbulk Ltd; The Vimeira* [1984] 2 Lloyd's Rep 66 at p. 75. **See also: concurrent hearing.**

consumer arbitrations - arbitrations between consumers and the traders, sometimes sponsored by the trade associations. **See: ABTA arbitration; British Telecom arbitration; Post Office arbitration; Personal Insurance Arbitration Service; National Small Claims Arbitration Service; Solicitors Arbitration Scheme.**

convention - a treaty, usually of a multilateral nature. **See: New York Convention 1958; European Convention on International Commercial Arbitration.**

convention award - an award made in pursuance of an arbitration agreement in the territory of a State, other than the United Kingdom which is a party to the New York Convention: *Section 7(1), Arbitration Act 1975.*

An award made in a foreign State irrespective of whether made before or after the foreign State has become a party to the New York Convention is enforceable in the United Kingdom as a convention award under section 3 of the Arbitration Act 1975: *Kuwait Minister of Public Works* v. *Sir Federick Snow & Partners (a firm) and others* [1983] 2 All ER 754 CA; [1984] 1 All ER 733 HL.

costs - the payment for legal services. In civil cases, the court has wide discretion in awarding costs. The general rule is that costs follow the event, i.e., the loser is to pay the costs of the winner. In party to party costs, the loser pays all costs reasonably and necessarily incurred by the winner. **See: party and party costs**

There is a taxing master who shall carry out taxation of costs if parties cannot agree upon the costs payable. **See: taxing master.**

In arbitration, the award of costs is up to the arbitrator's discretion: *Unimarine SA* v. *Canadian Transport Co Ltd; Canadian Transport Co Ltd* v. *AS Gerrards Rederi; AS Gerrards Rederi* v. *Ceres Hellenic Shipping Enterprises Ltd; The Catherine L* [1982] 1 Lloyd's Rep 484. However, the parties are free to agree as to costs, in spite of arbitrators having discretion to award costs: *Mansfield* v. *Robinson* [1928] 2 KB 353. Where it is provided that the arbitrator shall exercise his discretion in relation to award of costs, he ought to exercise this discretion: *re An Arbitration between Becker, Shillan & Co and Barry Brothers* [1921] 1 KB 391. The arbitrator's error in law or in fact regarding his discretion in awarding costs is not a ground for the court to set aside the award of costs: *Heaven & Kesterton Ltd* v. *Sven Widaeus A/B* [1958] 1 WLR 248. It is settled practice that, in the absence of special circumstancs, a successful party will receive his costs in arbitration, i.e., costs follow events: *Demolition & Construction Co Ltd* v. *Kent River Board* [1963] 2 Lloyd's Rep 7; *Dineen* v. *Walpole* [1969] 1 Lloyd's Rep 261. Where the arbitrator departs from the usual rule that costs follow the event, there is no duty of him to give reason: *Perry* v. *Stopher* [1959] 1 WLR 415. But generally, the arbitrator must give clear reasons for his award of costs when exercising his discretion: *Leif Hoegh & Co A/S* v. *Maritime Mineral Carriers Ltd; The Marques de Bolarque* [1982] 1 Lloyd's Rep 68.

costs follow the event - see: costs.

costs of the award - the fees payable to the arbitrator. The arbitrator can fix his own fees, provided that the fees are reasonable: *re An Arbitration between Stephens, Smith & Co and The Liverpool & London & Globe Insurance Co* (1892) 36 SJ 464. Otherwise, excessive charging by the arbitrator of the costs of the award may render the arbitrator guilty of misconduct: *Re An Arbitration between Prebble and Robinson & Another* [1892] 2 QB 602.

costs of the reference - all the costs of the arbitration reference, including the fees of the arbitrators. **See: costs; costs of the awards.**

costs on a common fund basis - formerly known as costs as between solicitors and client. These include all charges by the solicitor to his clients.

'(1) subject to subsection (2), any court in which a solicitor has been employed to prosecute or defend any suit, matter or proceedings may at any time - (a) declare the solicitor entitled to a charge on any property recovered or preserved through his instrumentality for his taxed costs in relation to that suit, matter or proceeding; and (b) make such orders for the taxation of those costs and for raising money to pay or for paying them out of the property recovered or preserved as the court think fit.

And all the conveyances and acts done to defeat, or operating to defeat, that charge shall, except in the case of a conveyance to a *bona fide* purchaser for value without notice, be void as against the solicitor.

(2) No order shall be made under subsection (1) if the right to recover the costs is barred by any statute of limitations': *Section 73, Solicitors Act 1974.*

In relation to arbitration, section 18(5) of the Arbitration Act 1950 provides that the power of the court before which any proceeding is being heard or is pending to charge property recovered or preserved in the proceeding with the payment of the solicitors' costs shall apply as if the arbitration were a proceeding in the High Court, and the High Court may make declaration and orders accordingly.

costs on trustee basis - all costs except where unreasonable in amount or unreasonably incurred.

costs thrown away - unnecessary costs incurred by a party arising from some procedural error committed by the other party. It may also be the costs which are properly incurred but wasted as a result of a subsequent act of the other party (e.g., by amending the pleadings).

counsel - a barrister or a collective term for barristers. **See also: advocates.**

counterclaim - an independent cause of action brought by cross-claim. **See also: claim.**

County Court - originally set up in 1846, this is now the civil law court in England and Wales governed by County Courts Act 1959. It has jurisdiction over actions in contract and tort within the amount of £5,000 claimed. While it possesses an extensive jurisdiction in actions concerning land, it also has jurisdiction in respect of divorce cases, which must be started in it. The County Court is presided by a circuit judge and a registrar. **See also: County Court arbitrations.**

County Court arbitrations - under sections 92 and 93 of the County Courts Act 1959, the County Court judge, with the consent of the parties, has power to order matter that comes before it to arbitration. This order is irrevocable except with the judge's consent. This power should be distinguished from the inherent jurisdiction of the High Court, as sections 92 and 93 apply only to proceedings which have been commenced in the County Court.

Court - a body established by law for the administration of justice by judges and magistrates.
  For the purposes of the Civil Evidence Act 1968, a court, in relation to an arbitration or reference, means the arbitrator or umpire and, in relation to proceedings before a tribunal (not being one of the ordinary courts of law), means the tribunal: *Section 18(2) Civil Evidence Act 1968.*

Court of Appeal - a part of the Supreme Court of Judicature which exercises appellate jurisdiction. It was created by the Judicature Acts 1873-75. Now, the court is divided into a Civil Division (presided over by the Master of the Rolls) and a Criminal Division (presided over by the Lord Chief Justice). In some cases, the Court of Appeal is the court of last resort but normally its decisions can be appealed to the House of Lords, either with its own leave or with leave of the House of Lords. The judges of the Court are known as the Lord Justices of Appeal. Puisne judges may also sit in the Court of Appeal by invitation.

No appeal shall lie to the Court of Appeal except as provided by the Arbitration Act 1979, from any decision of the High Court - (i) on an appeal under section 1 of that Act on a question of law arising out of an arbitration award; or (ii) under section 2 of that Act on a question of law arising in the course of a reference: *Section 18(1)(g), Supreme Court Act 1981.*

court of first instance -   (1) a court where proceedings are initiated; (2) generally a court where a case is tried rather than appealed to.

cross-appeals - appeals by both parties against the judgment of the lower courts, e.g., a buyer appeals against the judgment finding him liable to damages whilst the seller appeals against the same judgment on the ground that the amount of damages awarded is too low.

Crown Court - a part of the Supreme Court of Judicature with unlimited jurisdiction over all criminal cases. Created by the Courts Act 1971, it can sit at any centre in England and Wales designated by the Lord Chancellor. It is also an appellate court hearing appeals from Magistrates' Courts.

Crown privilege - the right of the Crown to withhold evidence in any legal proceeding on the ground of public interest. The claim of the privilege is subject to the scrutiny of the court which may reject it as unwarranted.

curial law - procedural law. **See: procedural law.**

customary manner, the - an agreement for arbitration 'in London according to British law in the customary manner' means an arbitration to be conducted in the usual manner for London arbitrations, namely, by an arbitrator for each side with an umpire if necessary': *Laertis Shipping Corpn* v. *Exportadora Espanola de Cementos Portland SA; The Laertis* [1982] 1 Lloyd's Rep 613.

D

Daily Cause List - see: **Cause List.**

damages - monetary compensation for breach of contract or a tort. The general rule is *restitutio in integram*, i.e., the plaintiff is entitled to full compensation. The recovery of damages for breach of contract is limited by rules relating to remoteness of damage and whether or not the plaintiff has taken all reasonable steps to mitigate his losses. Damages may be awarded as substantial or nominal damages. In the former case, it is awarded in accordance with the damage actually suffered. In the latter case, it is given where no damage has been caused, in order to vindicate the plaintiff's rights. Sometimes, damages are classified as liquidated or unliquidated damages. Unliquidated damages are damages fixed by the court while liquidated damages are pre-fixed by the parties in their contract. Damages may also be classified as general or special damages. **See also: exemplary damages.**

declaration - (1) a discretionary remedy given by the High Court regarding the rights and obligations of the parties. An arbitral award can also be a declaration; and (2) an oral or written statement not made on oath, which is nevertheless admissible as evidence as an exception to the rule of hearsay.

In arbitration, if the award is merely a declaration of the existence of the right of one party, that party may bring fresh proceedings in enforcing his right: *FJ Bloeman Pty Ltd* v. *Gold Coast City Council* [1973] AC 115.

decree-arbitral - the Scottish term for the arbiter's award or decision. It need not be in writing. But the most common practice is to present it in written form. It need not be in probative (witnessed) form as the submission. **See also: Books of Council and Session.**

Deed of Submission - term used in Scotland to denote the contract which the parties entered into to submit dispute to arbitration. **See also: arbitration agreement.**

default - failure to comply with mandatory rules of procedure. The plaintiff may obtain judgment in default if the defendant is in default and conversely, the defendant may appy to dismiss the action. **See also:** *ex parte* **proceeding.**

defendant - a person against whom actions are brought. **Compare: plaintiff, see also: respondent; defender.**

defender - the Scottish equivalent of respondent or defendant.

delay - **see: dilatoriness.**

deposit - a payment by one party to a contract to the other as a guarantee that the payee will perform the contract. This sum is normally forfeited if the payee fails to perform. In arbitration proceedings, it is normal for arbitral institutions to ask disputants to pay deposit to them before the proceedings commence.

differences - another term for disputes, although it is thought to be wider in scope than the latter. 'The word "differences" seems to me to be particularly apt for a case where the parties have not agreed': *Per* Danckwerks LJ in *F and G Sykes (Wessex) Ltd* v. *Fine Fare Ltd* [1967] 1 Lloyd's Rep 53 at p. 60.

dilatoriness - the act tending to, designed to cause, and/or given to delay. In the context of arbitration, 'if the party who initiated the event then withdraws or abandons his claim he must, at least *prima facie,* be taken to annul the event and to seek the cancellation of the arbitration in relation to the particular claim that constitutes the event. It may be that the other party will wish for a decision of the arbitrator, for there may be other claims which could be effected. On the other hand, he might gladly accept the position and consent to the arbitration being at an end. The fact that he has himself failed to proceed diligently with the appropriate steps in the arbitration will not prevent him from doing so. There is no implied term that he will not be dilatory. Lord Diplock made this clear for, as the Arbitration Act 1950 itself provided machinery to put an end to delay, there was no necessity to imply such a term'. *Per* Eveleigh LJ in *Andre & Cie SA* v. *Marine Transocean Ltd; The Splendid Sun* [1981] 2 All ER 993 CA at p. 1000.

Where parties to a reference act 'so tardily that it threatens to delay the hearing to a date when there will be a substantial risk that justice cannot be done, a necessary implication from the parties' having agreed that the arbitrator shall resolve their dispute that both parties, respondent as well as claimant, are under a mutual obligation to one another to join in in applying to the arbitrator for appropriate directions to put an end to the delay. Even if an application to the arbitrator for directions in such circumstances were a matter of right only and not, as I think it is, a mutual obligation, it provides a remedy to the party who thinks that the proceedings are not progressing fast enough voluntarily ...': *Per* Lord Diplock in *Bremer Vulkan Schiffbau und Maschinenfabrik* v.*South India Shipping Corpn* [1981] 1 All ER 289 HL at p. 301.

Delay in the proceedings does not amount to frustration of arbitration agreement: *Paal Wilson & Co A/S* v. *Partenereederi Hannah Blumenthal; The Hannah Blumenthal* [1983] 1 All ER 34 HL.

Delay in the proceedings cannot lead to mutual discharge of arbitration reference: *Allied Marine Transport Ltd* v. *Vale do Rio Doce Navegacao SA; The Leonidas D* [1985] 2 All ER 796 CA.

diligence - (1) execution and enforcement of a court's decree or a decree-arbitral in Scotland; and (2) process for recovering documents needed in evidence. Compare: discovery in English law. **See: discovery of document.**

direct examination - see: **examination-in-chief.**

discharge of contract - the end of contract either through performance or by express agreement of the parties, breach of contract or frustration of contract.

discontinuance of an action - a discontinuance of an action in the High Court within the time-limit does not bar a further action. The discontinuance of an action is by leave of the court. In arbitration, the discontinuance of an action must be consensual upon the agreement of both parties: *Allied Marine Transport Ltd* v. *Vale do Rio Doce Navegacao SA; The Leonidas D* [1983] 2 Lloyd's Rep 411. **See also: abandonment.**

discovery of document - the disclosure by one party to the other of documents in his possession, custody or power, relating to matters in question. In the High Court, this procedure is mutual and automatic. Where a party has reasons to believe that the other party has not disclosed fully the documents, he can apply for specific discovery.

In arbitration, unless otherwise agreed by the parties, discovery is not automatic and the arbitrator has no power to order discovery. The party, however, may apply to the High Court for such an order. Under section 12(6)(b) of the Arbitration Act 1950, the High Court shall have, for the purpose of and in relation to a reference, the same power of making orders in respect of discovery of documents.

discretion - the power of the court or arbitrators to take steps or make decisions as they think fit. Many rules of procedure are in discretionary form, e.g., the order for security for costs. **See: security for costs.**

disputants- a general term used to describe parties in an arbitration. Compare: litigants in an action in court. **See: litigants.**

doctrine of severability or separability - the principle that when the main or principal contract comes to an end, the arbitration clause contained therein is separable or severable and continues to be valid.

'I am ... of the opinion that what is commonly repudiation or total breach of contract, whether acquiesced in by the other party or not, does not abrogate the contract, though it may relieve the injured party of the duty of further fulfilling the obligations which he has by the contract undertaken to the repudiated party. The contract is not put out of existence, though all further performance of the obligations undertaken by each party in favour of the other may cease. It survives for the purpose of measuring the claims arising out of the breach and the arbitration clause survives for determining the mode of their settlement. The purposes of the contract have failed, but the arbitration clause is not one of the purposes of the contract': *Heyman and another* v. *Darwins Ltd* [1942] AC 356 HL. In reliance upon the authority of *Heyman* v. *Darwins Ltd,* Lord Diplock endorsed the view that an arbitration agreement would be severable from the main contract as a separate contract ancilliary to the main contract: **See:** *Bremer Vulkan Schiffbau und Maschinenfabrik* v. *South India Shipping Corpn Ltd* [1981] 2 WLR 141 HL; [1981] 1 All ER 289; [1980] 1 Lloyd's Rep 255. **See also: autonomy of the arbitration clause; arbitration agreement; void contract; voidable contract.**

document - written information in general. Documents used as evidence in court may include plans, drawings, photographs, books, maps, graphs, discs, tapes, soundtracks, negatives and films (see *section 10(1), Civil Evidence Act 1968).* There are other additional requirements attached to each type of documents in order that they may be admissible as evidence, e.g., a deed must be signed, sealed and delivered; a public document, such as an Act of Parliament, must be a government printer's copy; a byelaw of a local authority must be one certified by the clerk to the local authority.

documentary arbitration - an arbitration conducted on documents only. This is conducted where the sum in dispute is small, such that oral hearing is not called for, in order to minimise expenses, e.g., arbitration in connection with loss or damage of a letter or parcel. **(See: Post Office arbitration).** Under the Arbitration Rules of the Chartered Institute of Arbitrators, where the value of all matters in dispute between the parties does not exceed a certain amount, e.g., £5,000, the arbitrator may determine the dispute on the documents submitted to him by the parties, voluntarily or on his discretion, without any hearing. In some other arbitration schemes, e.g., the Arbitration Scheme for the Travel Industry, the scheme provides for arbitration on documents only. **See: ABTA arbitration.**

The parties may dispense with an oral hearing if they expressly agree to do so: *Oakland Metal Co Ltd* v. *Benaim & Co Ltd* [1953] 2

Lloyd's Rep 192 at p. 199. Otherwise, in the absence of agreement, a full oral hearing is presumed: *Altco Ltd* v. *Sutherland* [1971] 2 Lloyd's Rep 515.

documentary evidence - evidence contained in documents, which are submitted to prove certain fact in a hearing.

domestic arbitration agreement - an arbitration agreement which does not provide, expressly or by implication, for arbitration in a State other than the United Kingdom and to which neither - (a) an individual who is a national of, or habitually resident in, any State other than the United Kingdom; nor (b) a body corporate which is incorporated in, or whose central management and control is exercised in, any State other than the United Kingdom;
is a party at the time the proceedings are commenced: *Section 1(4), Arbitration Act 1975.*

Note: the definition of the 'domestic arbitration agreement' as provided in section 3(7) of the Arbitration Act 1979 is substantially identical to the above section 1(4) of the Arbitration Act 1975, except the last clause: '... is a party at the time the *arbitration agreement is entered into'*.

The bringing of an action in court in breach of a domestic arbitration agreement invokes the court to exercise its discretion to stay the proceedings: *Section 4(1), Arbitration Act 1950.* **See: stay of proceedings.**

E

enactment - an Act of Parliament, a Measure of the General Synod of the Church of England, an Order, or any other piece of subordinate legislation, or any particular provision contained in any of these, e.g., a particular section or article.

enforcement of arbitral award - there are two ways to enforce an arbitral award: (1) to register the award as a judgment of the High Court under section 26 of the Arbitration Act 1950; and (2) to bring an action on the award i.e., to take out a writ to sue on it. A failure to honour an award gives rise to an independent cause of action: *Agromet Motoimport Ltd* v. *Maulden Engineering Co (Beds) Ltd* [1985] 2 All ER 436. **See also: enforcement of judgment.**

enforcement of judgment - the process to enforce the court's order and decision. Judgment on money may be enforced by a number of methods, e.g., garnishee proceedings, charging orders, a writ of *fi-fa* (i.e., *fieri facias*) or warrant of execution in the County Court, a writ of sequestration, the appointment of a receiver, etc. In relation to injunction, a judgment may be enforced by order of committal or writ of sequestration.

entering an appearance - taking steps in giving notice of intention to defend an action. This includes applying for security for costs or delivering pleadings.

entering judgment - civil procedure where a judgment is formally recorded after it has been given by the court.

In respect of the judgment in the County Court, it is the court which draws it up and enters the judgment.

In respect of the judgment given by the Queen's Bench Division, it is the party which seeks to enter the judgment, draws it up and presents it with the pleadings and the certificate of the associate (clerk of the court) to an officer of the court for entry.

equitable - (1) reasonable, fair and just; and (2) a right recognised by the Court of Chancery.

equitable remedies - discretionary remedies granted under the principle of equity. They are: specific performance, rescission, cancellation, rectification, account, injunction, *Mareva* injunction, *Anton Piller* Order and the appointment of a receiver. Equitable remedies though discretionary, are nowadays mostly granted on authority. A party may seek these remedies in any division of the High Court and also in the County Court, where appropriate. However, arbitrators are not advised to exercise some of the remedies, such as specific performance, in view of their involvement of personal supervision, unless otherwise provided by the parties.

equity - (1) a share in a limited company; and (2) that part of English law which originated to supplement the rigidity of common law but remains a distinct class of its own. In the past, where litigants could not seek remedies under the jurisdiction of the common law courts, they could petition to the King, who relied on his Chancellor to dispense justice in each case. Thus, by the 15th century, equity began to be administered directly by the Lord Chancellor and later by the Court of Chancery. It thus developed as a distinct class of law from those growing up in the common law courts. Two maxims illustrate equity vividly: *he who comes to equity must come with clean hands; equity varied with the length of the Chancellor's foot.*

Under the Judicature Acts 1873-75, where equity is in conflict with rules of law, equity is to prevail.

Equity, though still discretionary in nature, is now administered upon established precedents. **See: equitable remedies.**

In arbitration, where parties agree that the arbitrator shall decide *ex aequo et bono,* he is at liberty to decide the dispute submitted to him in accordance with the principles of fairness and justice, akin to the equity in English law when it was first developed. **See: *ex aequo et bono; amiable compositeur.***

error - a mistake of law in a judgment or order of a court or an award of an arbitral tribunal or in some procedural steps in legal proceedings.

error of law on the face of the award - a mistake of law, which is apparent on the document of award, in the arbitrator's decision. By virtue of section 1(1) of the Arbitration Act 1979, such an error is no longer a ground for the court to set aside or remit the award.

essential features of a judge or arbitrator - '(a) there is a dispute or a difference between the parties which has been formulated in some way or another; (b) the dispute or difference has been remitted by the parties to the person to resolve in such a manner that he is called on to exercise a judicial function; (c) where appropriate the parties must have been provided with an opportunity to present evidence and/or submissions in support of their respective claims in the dispute; and (d) the parties have agreed to accept his decision.' *Per* Lord Wheatley in *Arenson* v. *Casson Beckman Rutley & Co* [1975] 3 All ER 901 at pp. 915-916.

European Convention on International Commercial Arbitration - also known as the Geneva Convention of 1961. Done at Geneva on 21 April 1961 and came into force on 7 January 1964 in accordance with paragraph 8 of Article 10, with the exception of paragraphs 3 to 7 of Article 4, which came into force on 18 October 1965, in accordance with paragraph 4 of the Annex to the Convention.
This Convention shall apply:- (a) to arbitration agreements concluded for the purpose of settling disputes arising from international trade between physical or legal persons having, when concluding the agreement, their habitual place of residence or their seat in different contracting states; (b) to arbitral procedures and awards based on agreements referred to in paragraph (a) above: *Article 1 European Convention on International Commercial Arbitration*.
The United Kingdom is not a signatory state to this Convention.

evidence - testimony, document, map, etc., which is admissible by the court or tribunal to prove the existence or non-existence of certain facts.

The law of evidence is a collection of rules governing the presentation of facts and proof in proceedings in court. Arbitration references are not governed by the strict rules of evidence as in actions in court, unless otherwise agreed by the parties.

ex aequo et bono - a Latin phrase meaning as a result of fair dealing and good conscience or good faith, i.e., on the basis of natural justice or equity. See: *amiable compositeur; equity.*

ex parte - on behalf of.

ex parte **proceeding** - the default proceeding when one party is absent from the hearing. In relation to arbitration proceeding, where one party is obstructive and refuses to carry out his obligation to submit to arbitration, the arbitrator may proceed *ex parte,* i.e., in the absence of the obstructive party: *Waller* v. *King* (1723) 9 Mod Rep 63. But the arbitrator must give summary notice to all parties: *Gladwin* v. *Chilcote* (1841) 9 Dowl 550; Woll 189; 5 JP 531. Failure to give clear warning of an *ex parte* proceeding will render the arbitrator guilty of misconduct and the award be set aside: *The Myron (Owner)* v. *Tradex Export SA* [1969] 1 Lloyd's Rep 411.

Now, in pursuance of an order made by the High Court under section 5(2) of the Arbitration Act 1979, the arbitrator or umpire shall have power to proceed an *ex parte* reference in like manner as a judge of the High Court might continue with proceedings in that court. No warning to the parties in this respect is needed.

An *ex parte* award is as binding as an award made when all parties to the dispute have been present at the reference.

examination - the giving of evidence through questioning of a witness on oath or affirmation. The procedure on examination of a witness may consist of examination-in-chief, cross-examination and re-examination. Where there is an oral hearing in an arbitration reference, examination of witnesses is a normal procedure. See: **witness.**

examination-in-chief - also known as direct examination. This is the procedure in a hearing where the witness is examined by the party which calls him.

exclusion agreement - a written agreement to exclude the right of appeal to the court against the arbitral award or on any point of law. Formerly, agreement purported to oust the jurisdiction of the court to supervise the way in which arbitrators apply the law in reaching their awards was void as being contrary to public policy: *Czarnikow* v. *Roth Schmidt & Co* [1922] 2 KB 478; [1922] All ER Rep 45. But now the validity of such an agreement is fortified by section 3 of the Arbitration Act 1979 subject to some special limitations imposed under section 4 of the 1979 Act. The court has recently endorsed this type of agreement in *Pioneer Shipping Ltd and others* v. *BTP Tioxide Ltd; The Nema* [1981] 2 All ER 1030 at p. 1038; *Arab African Energy Corpn Ltd* v. *Olieproduckten Nederland B V* [1983] 2 Lloyd's Rep 419 at p. 423; In *Marine Contractors Inc* v. *Shell Petroleum Development Co of Nigeria Ltd,* 27 BLR 131 at p. 133, the court held that the exclusion agreement applied to interim award. Where parties agree to hold arbitration under certain institutional rules which exclude the right to appeal, this amounts to a valid exclusion agreement, under section 3(1) of the Arbitration Act 1979: *Arab African Energy Corpn Ltd* v. *Olieproduckten Nederland BV* [1983] 2 Lloyd's Rep 419.

In relation to exclusion agreements touching on special category contracts viz., maritime, insurance and commodity contracts, these agreements will not have effect unless they have been entered into *after* the commencement of the arbitration reference: *Section 4(1)(c)(i), Arbitration Act 1979;* or if the arbitration concerns a contract expressly provided for it to be governed by law other than English and Welsh law: *Section 4(1)(c)(ii), Arbitration Act 1979* .

An enclusion agreement shall be of no effect in relation to an award made on, or a question of law arising in the course of a reference under, an arbitration agreement which is a domestic arbitration agreement **(see: domestic arbitration agreement)** unless the exclusion agreement is entered into after the commencement of the arbitration in which the award is made or, as the case may be, in which the question of law arises: *Section 3(6), Arbitration Act 1979.*

exemplary damages - also known as punitive or vindictive damages. These are damages given as punishment rather than compensation. Thus, they cannot be awarded for breach of contract. **See: damages.**

exhibit - an object or document shown to the witness to support the evidence of the witness in a hearing.

Expedited Form - Form 10 of the Appendix A in Part 2 of the Supreme Court Practice for the use of all applications in relation to Arbitration Acts 1950-1979 by originating summons. These include the following applications:- (a) to appoint an arbitrator or umpire under section 10 of the Arbitration Act 1950; (b) for interlocutory relief under section 12(6) of the Arbitration Act 1950; (c) to revoke the authority of an arbitrator or for an order that an arbitration agreement shall cease to have effect in cases involving fraud, under section 24(1) of the Arbitration Act 1950; and (d) for an order for extension of time to commence arbitration proceedings, under section 27, Arbitration Act 1950. **See also: originating summons.**

expert arbitrator - an arbitrator who is an expert himself, appointed to sit in a specialised or technical arbitration. He is appointed as arbitrator because of his expertise in certain fields which are relevant to the disputes under reference. However, even though he is an expert himself, he is not permitted to use his own knowledge in the reference, such as to substitute it for the evidence of the parties.
'His [the expert arbitrator's] function is not to supply evidence for the defendants but to adjudicate upon the evidence given before him. He can and should use his special knowledge so as to understand the evidence that is given - the letters that have passed - the usage of the trade - the dealings in the market - and to appreciate the worth of all that he sees upon a view. But he cannot use his special knowledge - or at any rate he should not use it - so as to provide evidence on behalf of the defendants which they have not chosen to provide for themselves. For then he would be discarding the role of an impartial arbitrator ... . At any rate he should not use his own knowledge ... without putting his own knowledge to them and giving them a chance of answering it and

showing that his own view is wrong.' *Per* Lord Denning in *A Fox* v. *P G Wellfair Ltd* [1981] 2 Lloyd's Rep 514 at p. 522.

'... an expert arbitrator should not in effect give evidence to himself without disclosing the evidence on which he relies to the parties ... He should not act on his private opinion without disclosing it. It is undoubtedly true that an expert arbitrator can use his own expert knowledge. But a distinction is made in the cases between general expert knowledge and knowledge of special facts relevant to the particular case ... If the expert arbitrator, as he may be entitled to do, forms a view of the facts different from that given in the evidence which might produce a contrary result to that which emerges from the evidence then he should bring that view to the attention of the parties.' *Per* Dunn LJ in *A Fox* v. *P G Wellfair Ltd* (*ibid.*). **See also: expert knowledge of the arbitrator.**

expert evidence - the submission of evidence by an expert, normally evidence of opinion on matters in which he claims to be an expert. In relation to an arbitration reference, the arbitrator dictates the method of giving such evidence and its admissibility. Where the parties opt for the conduct of the arbitration to be subject to strict rules of evidence, the admissibility of the expert evidence is subject to the Civil Evidence Act 1972 and the rules of court made under it: *Section 5(2), Civil Evidence Act 1972.*

Under Part IV of RSC Order 38, except with the leave of the arbitrator, or where the parties agree, no expert evidence may be adduced at the reference, unless the party seeking to adduce it has applied to the arbitrator to determine whether a direction should be given for the substance of the evidence to be disclosed to the other party in the form of a written report.

expert knowledge of the arbitrator - where an arbitrator is an expert himself appointed to the tribunal to conduct the reference by virtue of his being an expert, he is generally permitted to use his expert knowledge in a general sense. **(See: expert arbitrator).** '... There is an unavoidable inclination to rely on one's own expertise ... and a very large part of the reason why an arbitrator with expert qualifications is chosen. Nevertheless, the rules of natural justice do require, ... that matters which are likely to form the subject of decision, ... should be exposed for the comments and submissions of the parties. ... It is not right that a decision should be based on specific matters which the parties have never had the chance to deal with, nor is it right that a party should first learn of adverse points in the decision against him': *Per* Bingham J in *Zermalt Holdings SA* v. *Nu-Life Upholstery Repairs Ltd* (1985) 275 Estates Gazette 1134 at p. 1138. Any use of expert knowledge by the arbitrator in relation to the matter in dispute must be disclosed to the parties so as to give them the opportunity of challenging the arbitrator's expert knowledge. Otherwise, it will be misconduct on the part of the arbitrator to rely on his own expert knowledge to arrive at conclusion and award: *A Fox* v. *P G Wellfair Ltd* [1981] 2 Lloyd's 514 CA. **See also: expert arbitrator.**

expert witness - a witness who is called to testify before an action or arbitration reference by virtue of the fact that he is an expert in his profession or his field of specialisation. Expert witness, as distinct from an ordinary witness, is entitled to state his opinion on matters in which he is an expert, if asked for, in addition to giving statement of facts.

extension of time - where the terms of an agreement to refer future disputes to arbitration provide that any claim to which the agreement applies shall be barred unless notice to appoint an arbitrator is given or an arbitrator is appointed or some other step to commence arbitration proceedings is taken within a time fixed by the agreement, and a dispute arises to which the agreement applies, the High Court, if it is of opinion that in the circumstances of the case undue hardship would otherwise be caused, and notwithstanding that the time so fixed has expired, may, on such terms, if any, as the justice of the case may require, but without prejudice to the provisions of any enactment limiting the time for the commencement of arbitration proceedings, extend the time for such period as it thinks proper: *Section 27, Arbitration Act 1950.*

In deciding whether to extend time or not, the Court should look at all the relevant circumstances of the particular case. In particular, the following matters should be considered :- (a) the length of the delay; (b) amount at stake; (c) whether the delay was due to the fault of the claimant or to circumstances outside his control; (d) if it was due to the fault of the claimant, the degree of such fault; (e) whether the claimant was misled by the other party; and (f) whether the other party has been prejudiced by the delay, and if so, the degree of such prejudice.

'I think it is right to give the word "claim" in the section (i.e., section 27) a wide and liberal interpretation. In my judgment, any claim to have determined by arbitration a matter in issue between the parties on which the rights of the party making the claim depend is a claim within the meaning of the section.' *Per* Bridge LJ in *Sioux Inc* v. *China Salvage Co; Kwangchow Branch and another; The American Sioux* [1980] 3 All ER 154 at p. 159.

'[Section 27] does not empower the court to extend a time limit for commencing arbitration if, in the absence of such an extension, the claim would remain alive and could be litigated, as was the case, for example, in *Pinnock Bros* v. *Lewis & Peat Ltd* [1923] 1 KB 690'. *Per* Donaldson LJ in *Babanaft International Co SA* v. *Avant Petroleum Inc; The Oltenia* [1982] 3 All ER 244 at p. 255.

An application for extension of time-limit under section 27 must be made promptly: *Richmond Shipping Ltd* v. *Agro Co of Canada Ltd* [1973] 2 Lloyd's Rep 145; the making of a claim in writing can be 'some other step to commence arbitration proceedings' within section 27: *Jedranska Slobodna Plovidba* v. *Oleagine SA; The Luka Botic* [1983] 3 All ER 602. 'Section 27 of the Arbitration Act 1950 applies whenever the terms of an agreement provide that "any claim to which the agreement applies shall be barred" unless notice is given etc. ... Section 27 applies ... whether under the Centrocon charterparty or Article III, r. 6, of the Hague Rules, or otherwise.' *Per* Lord Denning MR in *Consolidated Investment & Contracting Co* v. *Saponaria Shipping Co Ltd; The Virgo* [1978] 3 All ER 988 at p. 991. **See also: Centrocon arbitration clause.**

'The whole object of the section (i.e., section 27) was to provide discretion in the court to relieve people from the hardship which had been caused or was being caused by clauses of a very similar type to Article III, r. 6, of the Hague Rules, which also purported to bar the right.' : *Per* Kerr J in *The Angeliki* [1973] 2 Lloyd's Rep 226 at p. 229.

See generally: **Atlantic Shipping Clause.**

F

fact - an event or state of affairs proved to have happened or existed.

facts in issue - (1) facts which the party must prove in order to succeed; (2) subordinate or collateral facts which the party must prove in order to succeed, e.g., the admissibility of evidence or the credibility of witness.

failure to make discovery - a party's failure to produce documents for inspection. Under section 12(6)(b) of the Arbitration Act 1950, the High Court shall have, for the purpose of and in relation to a reference, the same power of making orders in respect of discovery of documents. **See: discovery of documents.**

FCIArb - Fellow of the Chartered Institute of Arbitrators. **See also: Chartered Institute of Arbitrators, the.**

Federation of Oils, Seeds and Fats Association - **See: FOSFA.**

fieri facias - also known as *fi fa.* A Latin phrase which means you should cause it to be made. In court action, *fi fa* is a writ of execution to enforce the judgment of debt or damages.

final award - the award, of the arbitrator or of the arbitral institution, to which the parties have submitted their disputes for determination, delivered at the end of the hearing. Contrast: **interim award.** Unless a contrary intention is expressed therein, every arbitration agreement shall, where such a provision is applicable to the reference, be deemed to contain a provision that the award to be made by the arbitrator or umpire shall be final and binding on the parties and the persons claiming under them respectively: *Section 16, Arbitration Act 1950.* **See also: award; appeal;** *Nema* **Guidelines, the.** Unless a contrary intention is expressed in the arbitration agreement, the arbitrator may make one or more final awards in his disposition of the various matters referred to him: *Wrightson* v. *Bywater and others* (1838) 7 LJ Ex 83. **See also: interim award.**

final judgment - the judgment of the court that ends an action. It can be appealed against without leave of the court. **Compare: interlocutory judgment.**

foreign arbitration - an arbitration which is held in England under English law but involves parties who are not nationals of, or habitually resident in the United Kingdom; or if the parties are bodies corporate, they are not incorporated in or their central management and control is not exercised in the United Kingdom.

In respect of a foreign arbitration held in England, the court may not grant a stay of proceedings, if one party commences actions in court: *Section 1(2), Arbitration Act 1975.* **See: stay of proceedings; domestic arbitration agreement.**

However, foreign arbitration held in England in the absence of express provisions, is subject to English procedural law: *Bank Mellat* v. *Helliniki Techniki SA* [1983] 3 All ER 428 CA, and the award of such an arbitration is an English award, which may be enforced in the same manner as a judgment under section 26 of the Arbitration Act 1950.

In Scotland, any arbitration applying the law other than Scots law is termed foreign arbitration.

foreign award - an award delivered by arbitral tribunal or arbitral institution after an arbitration reference held outside the United Kingdom. If it is a convention award, it may be enforced in England and Wales under section 26, Arbitration Act 1950 by virtue of section 3, Arbitration Act 1975. **See also: convention award.**

foreign law - in relation to English private international law, any legal system besides English. Thus Scots law, the law of Northern Ireland, the Channel Islands and Isle of Man are, for the purposes of English private international law, foreign law.

Where an element of foreign law arises in English law, it is usually treated as a question of fact, which must be proved in each case.

In relation to arbitration, where the rules governing the conflict of laws indicate that the substance of the dispute is governed by foreign law, the arbitrator must apply that law. However, English rule of procedure assumes foreign law to be the same as English law, unless otherwise proved. Thus, arbitrator's decision on foreign law, which is a matter of fact, is not open to appeal.

forum - from Latin, meaning public place. The place or country where a case is being heard. **See: *lex fori; lex arbitri.***

FOSFA - Federation of Oils, Seeds and Fats Association, formed in 1971 in London by the amalgamation of the Incorporated Oil & Seeds Association, the London Oil & Tallow Trade Association, the London Copra Association and the Seed, Oil, Cake & General Produce Association. FOSFA has over 500 members from about 40 countries. The members are producers, shippers, merchants brokers, crushers, refiners, companies providing superintending services, laboratories and others involved in various ways in the trade.

FOSFA International as it is now known, conducts and supervises commodity arbitrations in relation to trade. Its arbitration set-up is two-tier, maintaining a forum for reference in the first instance and an appeal board.

FOSFA arbitrations in the first instance are conducted in pursuance of the arbitration clauses contained in its various standard forms. A FOSFA arbitration tribunal consists of two arbitrators and an umpire, who is nominated by the Association. Where disputants are dissatisfied with the award of the tribunal, they can apply for the award to be reviewed by the Association's own Boards of Appeal. Under certain circumstances, the parties may also appeal to the Court against the decision of the FOSFA Board of Appeal. **See: FOSFA Board of Appeal.**

FOSFA arbitration clause - any dispute arising out of a contract subject to FOSFA Rules, including any question of law arising in connection therewith, shall be referred to arbitration in London (or elsewhere if so agreed).

FOSFA Board of Appeal - within 42 days after an award is delivered by the arbitration tribunal set up under the FOSFA Rules, a dissatisfied party to the arbitration may appeal against the award to the FOSFA Board of Appeal, which consists of five members elected and appointed from the Committee of Appeal. No counsel or solicitors are allowed to represent the parties unless with the approval of the Board. Under the current Rules, a person who has acted as an arbitrator in an arbitration will be disqualified to sit in the Board of Appeal on the same case. No award of a Board of Appeal shall be questioned or invalidated on the ground of any irregularity in the election of the Board of Appeal or of any of its members or on the ground that any member of the Board was not eligible to serve, unless objection is made in writing and established to the satisfaction of the Council of the FOSFA before the hearing of the appeal has commenced.

The Board of Appeal shall confirm the award appealed against unless at least three of the members of the Board decide to vary the award. The award of the Board shall be final and binding unless a special case (**see: case stated; special case procedure**) has been stated for the opinion of the court. **See: FOSFA arbitration.**

frustration - 'the doctrine of frustration has been developed as a judicial device to relieve a contracting party in certain limited circumstances where it would be harsh to hold him to the apparent terms of the contract. It applies when circumstances have so radically altered from the state of things when the contract was made that the court can say that the parties cannot have intended their contractual obligations to apply in such altered circumstances. In all the cases to which the doctrine has been applied it is possible to point to some supervening event which has had a catastrophic effect on the contract and has occurred without the fault of the parties. Examples ... include the outbreak of war, the cancellation of an expected event, the destruction of the object that was the subject matter of the contract, seizure of a ship by foreign government, an explosion and so forth ... in every case the delay has been due to some unexpected external cause beyond the control of the parties ...' : *Per* Griffiths LJ in *Paal Wilson & Co A/S* v. *Partenreederei Hannah Blumenthal; The Hannah Blumenthal* [1982] 3 All ER 394 CA at p. 406. 'The essence of "frustration" is that it should not be due to the act or election of the party.'*: Per* Lord Wright in *Maritime National Fish Ltd* v. *Ocean Trawlers Ltd* [1935] AC 524 at p. 530; [1935] All ER Rep 86 at p. 89.

In the context of arbitration, the doctrine has no application and cannot be invoked by a contracting party when the frustrating event was at all times within his control; still less can it apply in a situation in which the parties owed a contractual duty to one another to prevent the frustrating event occurring: *Paal Wilson & Co A/S* v. *Partenreederei Hannah Blumenthal; The Hannah Blumenthal (ibid.).*

Furthermore, the parties' delay in proceeding with the arbitration resulted in an inability to obtain a 'satisfactory trial' because of the difficulty which the arbitral tribunal will encounter in ascertaining the true facts, is not capable in law of bringing an arbitration agreement to an end by frustration: *Paal Wilson & Co A/S* v. *Partenreederei Hannah Blumenthal ; The Hannah Blumenthal* [1983] 1 All ER 34 HL. **See also: frustration delay.**

frustration delay - the delay of a contracting party in carrying out his obligation under a contract is so grave as to enable the other party to rescind: See the judgment of Devlin LJ in *Universal Cargo Carriers Corpn* v. *Citati* [1957] 2 All ER 70; [1957] 2 QB 401. **See also: frustration.**

functus officio - having discharged his duty. In relation to arbitrators, the term is used nowadays to describe the position of an arbitrator once he has made his award.

As regards the effect of remission of the award under section 22 of the Arbitration Act 1950, on the jurisdiction of the arbitrator, '... the arbitration tribunal becomes *functus officio* upon the making of the award; and the effect of the remission is to revive their jurisdiction. But their jurisdiction is ... not necessarily revived in its entirety. The extent to which it is revived will depend upon the order of the court. Where, for example, an award is remitted to an arbitrator to reconsider one of the matters referred, the court may, by its order for remission, expressly or impliedly restrict the revival of the arbitrator's jurisdiction in respect of that particular matter. Likewise, where an award is remitted for the arbitrator to reconsider a particular aspect of a matter referred, then the court may, expressly or impliedly, restrict the revival of the arbitrator's jurisdiction to the reconsideration of that particular aspect. So, for example, where an award is remitted for an arbitrator to correct an admitted mistake in his award, his jurisdiction will generally only be revived so far as is necessary for him to make that correction, but no more.' *Per* Ackner LJ in *Interbulk Ltd* v. *Aiden Shipping Co Ltd; The Vimeira (No.1)* [1985] 2 Lloyd's Rep 410 at p. 411.

G

GAFTA - Grain and Feed Trade Association Ltd, London. A trade organisation formed in 1971 by the amalgamation of the London Corn Trade Association and the Cattle Food Trade Association (Incorporated). The membership of the GAFTA includes producers, shippers, traders, millers, feed merchants, companies with superintending services, arbitrators and others. GAFTA provides, *inter alia*, the trade with arbitration services. Its arbitral structure provides for an arbitration reference of the first instance with possible review by its Boards of Appeal constituted by the associations. **See: GAFTA Board of Appeal.**

GAFTA arbitration clause - '(a) any dispute arising out of or under this contract shall be settled by arbitration in accordance with the Arbitration Rules, No. 125, of the Grain and Feed Trade Association Limited, in the edition current at the date of this contract, such Rules forming part of this contract and of which both parties hereto shall be deemed to be cognisant; (b) neither party hereto, nor any persons claiming under either of them shall bring any action or other legal proceedings against the other of them in respect of any such dispute until such dispute shall first have been heard and determined by the arbitrator(s) or a Board of Appeal, as the case may be, in accordance with the Arbitration Rules and it is expressly agreed and declared that the obtaining of an award from the arbitrator(s) or a Board of Appeal, as the case may be, shall be a condition precedent to the right of either party hereto or of any person claiming under either of them to bring any action or other legal proceedings against the other of them in respect of any such dispute.' **See also:** *Scott* **v.** *Avery* **clause.**

GAFTA Board of Appeal - GAFTA operates an appeal machinery for the dissatisfied parties to a GAFTA arbitration. The Board of Appeal is formed by five members who are elected by postal ballot from one of the standing committees of appeal. These standing committees are elected annually by the GAFTA Council. The appeal may be a new trial wherein fresh evidence may be submitted. No legally qualified advocate, barrister or solicitor may represent the parties unless with leave of the Board. The decision of the Board to confirm, vary or set aside the award of the arbitrator in the arbitration of the first instance, is final and conclusive. But the GAFTA Rules permit the parties to appeal to the court on questions of law even after the Board has delivered its decision. **See also: GAFTA; case stated; special case procedure.**

garnishee - a person who has been ordered by the court to pay a debt to a third party. For example, a bank is ordered to pay 'C', a judgment creditor out of 'D's' , the judgment debtor's account. **See: garnishee proceedings.**

garnishee proceedings - actions in court initiated by the judgment creditor to seek the order of the court to order a third party other than the judgment debtor, to pay the judgment debt.

'Gencon' Charterparty - a commonly used standard form of voyage charterparty. Among the many terms and conditions, it contains an arbitration clause.

Grain and Feed Trade Association Ltd, London - See: **GAFTA.**

H

Hague Conventions for the Pacific Settlement of International Disputes - a series of international conventions held at The Hague from 1899 to 1907 regarding war. The 1899 Convention established a Permanent Court of Arbitration. **See: Permanent Court of Arbitration.**

Hague Rules - A set of rules relating to bills of lading formulated in September 1921 at a meeting of the International Law Association at The Hague. In 1924, the Hague Rules became an international convention. In the United Kingdom, the Rules have been given force by virtue of the Carriage of Goods by Sea Act 1924. The Rules are now superseded by the Hague-Visby Rules, which have been given force by the Carriage of Goods by Sea Act 1971. **See: Hague-Visby Rules.**

Hague-Visby Rules - the amending rules of the Hague Rules by a protocol signed in Brussels in February 1968. Since the United Kingdom was a signatory to the protocol, Parliament passed the Carriage of Goods by Sea Act 1971 so as to give the Rules effect in the United Kingdom.

hearing - a trial or motion, which is normally oral, for judgment. **See also: oral hearing.**

hearsay evidence - an oral or written evidence tendered by a person who is not called as witness to be examined in a hearing. The evidence is submitted to the court by another as proof of the matters stated therein. Generally, hearsay evidence is inadmissible, but there are many exceptions to this rule.

High Court of Justice - established by the Judicature Acts 1873-75 as a constituent part of the Supreme Court of Judicature. It consists of three divisions: The Queen's Bench Division, Chancery Division and Family Division. In respect of its supervisory role on arbitration where the Arbitration Acts 1950-1979 apply, it is exercised by the Queen's Bench Division. In relation to commercial arbitration, it comes within the jurisdiction of the Commercial Court of the Queen's Bench Division. **See: Commercial Court.**

HL - House of Lords. **See: House of Lords; Lords of Appeal in Ordinary; appeal; Law Lords.**

House of Lords - The Upper House of the British Parliament consisting of Lords Spiritual and Lords Temporal. The Lords Spiritual are the two archbishops and senior bishops of the Church of England. The Lords Temporal are peers and peeresses in their own right and the life peers and peeresses (**See:** *sections 4 and 6, Peerage Act 1963*) and the Lords of Appeal in Ordinary (Law Lords). The Lord Chancellor is the Speaker and President of the House. The House has judicial and legislative roles in the British Constitutional convention.

In respect of judicial function, the House is the final court of appeal in the United Kingdom. The appeals are heard by the Appellate Committee consisting of three to five Lords of Appeal in Ordinary. The decision of the House is represented by the majority opinion of the Appellate Committee. **See also: Lords of Appeal in Ordinary; leapfrog procedure; appeal.**

I

ICC - International Chamber of Commerce, headquarters in Paris. **See: ICC arbitration.**

ICC arbitration - an arbitration held under the ICC Arbitration Rules. Thus, it is administered and supervised by the ICC Court of Arbitration. The Court which functions through the ICC Secretariat in Paris will examine and approve the application for arbitration under its rules. Where the Court is satisfied that the case may proceed to arbitration it will nominate such a case to the various ICC national committees which will then recommend arbitrators to form an arbitration tribunal to conduct the reference. The resultant award is subject to the scrutiny and approval of the ICC Court in Paris before it is published and notified to the parties.

    Although the ICC has its headquarters in France, ICC arbitrations may be held elsewhere. Thus, its award is not necessarily French, but is an award of the place where the arbitration is held, e.g., the award of an ICC arbitration held in London is an English award.

ICC arbitration clause - 'all disputes arising in connection with the present contract shall be finally settled under the Rules of Conciliation and Arbitration of the International Chamber of Commerce by one or more arbitrators appointed in accordance with the said Rules.'

    Attention is called to the fact that the laws of certain countries require that parties to contracts expressly accept arbitration clause sometimes in a precise and particular manner.

    The parties may - if they so desire - stipulate in the arbitration clause itself the national law applicable to the contract. The parties' free choice of the place of arbitration is not limited by the ICC.

ICCA - International Council for Commercial Arbitration.

ICJ - International Court of Justice. **See: International Court of Justice.**

ICSID - International Centre for Settlement of Investment Disputes. See: **International Centre for Settlement of Investment Disputes.**

immunity from suit - generally, the exemption from legal actions '... the undoubted rule, based on public policy that a judge is not liable in damages for negligence in performing his judicial duties. The next ... is that those employed to perform duties of a judicial character are not liable to their employers for negligence. This rule has been applied to arbitrators for a very long time. It is firmly established and could not now be questioned ...' *Per* Lord Reid in *Sutcliffe* v. *Thackrah* [1974] 1 All ER 859 at p. 862; [1974] AC 727 at p. 735; [1974] 2 WLR 295 at p. 297. An arbitrator's immunity is exceptional to the general rule of liability for negligence: *Per* Lord Simon of Glaisdale in *Arenson* v. *Casson Beckman Rutley &Co* [1977] AC 405 at p. 419; [1975] 3 All ER 901 at p. 907.

impartiality of arbitrator - where impartiality of the arbitrator is put to question and proven to be otherwise, such that he has misconducted himself or the proceedings, on application by the party, the court may remove him: *Section 23(1), Arbitration Act 1950.* The court has also power to give relief where an arbitrator is not impartial, e.g., to order that the arbitration agreement shall cease to have effect or to give leave to revoke the authority of the arbitrator or to refuse to stay any action brought in breach of the agreement: *Section 24(3), Arbitration Act 1950.*

imputed bias - '[this] arises when the relationship between the arbitrator and the parties, or between the arbitrator and the subject-matter of the dispute is such as to create the risk that he will be incapable of acting impartially.' *Per* Ackner LJ in *Bremer Handelsgesellschaft mbH* v. *Ets Soules et Cie and Anthony G Scott* [1985] 2 Lloyd's Rep 199 at p. 201, CA.

    The test of 'imputed bias' is an objective one i.e., whether ... there exists grounds from which a reasonable person would think that there was a real likelihood that (the arbitrator) could not, or would not, fairly determine ... the issue on the basis of the evidence and arguments to be adduced before him: *Hagop Ardahalian* v. *Unifert International*

SA; The Elissar [1984] 2 Lloyd's Rep 84 at p. 89. The reasonable man forms his view 'with no inside knowledge': *Per* Cross LJ in *Hannam v. Bradford Corporation* [1970] 1 WLR 937 at p. 949. The reference to 'no inside knowledge' is that of the character of the persons who are being accused of bias: *Per* Mustill J in *Bremer Handelsgesellschaft mbH* v. *Ets Soules et Cie and Anthony G Scott* [1985] 1 Lloyd's Rep 160 at p. 168. The degree of probability needed to found a charge of imputed bias is reasonable suspicion of bias: *Per* Staughton J in *Tracomin SA* v. *Gibbs Nathaniel (Canada) Ltd & George Jacob Bridge* [1985] 1 Lloyd's Rep 586.

in camera - in the Chamber (Latin). In private. Arbitration proceedings are normally held *in camera* unless otherwise agreed by the parties. No unauthorised person or public may be present at the arbitration reference. **See also: private arbitration.**

incapable of being performed - as contained in section 1(1) of the Arbitration Act 1975 'should be construed as referring only to the question whether an arbitration agreement is capable of being performed up to the stage when it results in an award; and should not be construed as extending to the question whether, once an award has been made, the party against whom it is made will be capable of satisfying it. ... the fact that, if an award were made against one party, he would be incapable of satisfying it, would not necessarily mean that the arbitration agreement was incapable of being performed.' : *Per* Brandon J in *The Rena K* [1979] QB 377 at p. 393; [1978] 1 Lloyd's Rep 545 at pp. 552 - 553.

in extenso - at full length.

in personam - (of an act or proceeding). One concerning, with reference to, or available against, a specific person, as opposed to *in rem.*

in re - in the matter of (Latin). A phrase which is normally used to cite the reference of the law report pertaining to arbitration, e.g., *In re An*

Arbitration between Montgomery, Jones & Co (1898) 78 LT NS 406. It is often abbreviated to *re*.

in rem - an act, proceeding or right against the world at large, as opposed to *in personam*. In maritime arbitration, if a party obtains an award in his favour and the opposite party is unable to satisfy it, the winning party is entitled to have the stay of the action removed and to proceed to a judgment *in rem* in it. 'It follows, in my view that a cause of action *in rem* does not, as a matter of law, become merged in an arbitral award ...': *Per* Brandon J in *The Rena K* [1978] 1 Lloyd's Rep 545 at p. 560. See also, *The Tuyuti* [1984] 2 All ER 545 CA.

in toto - entirely, wholly.

incorporation of arbitration clause - an arbitration clause can be incorporated into another contract, e.g., an arbitration clause in a charterparty can be incorporated into the bill of lading. However, mere reference that it is to be incorporated is not sufficient, more specific and distinct words are needed: *T W Thomas & Co Ltd* v. *Portsea Steamship Co Ltd* [1912] AC 1, HL; *The Phonizien* [1966] 1 Lloyd's Rep 150; *The Rena K* [1979] 1 All ER 397.

Constructive notice of incorporation of arbitration clause does not in effect incorporate the arbitration clause into the charterparty: *The Njegos* [1935] All ER Rep 863.

industrial arbitration - a reference to ascertain and declare but not to enforce the respective rights and liabilities of the parties. Hence, this type of arbitration is non-judicial: *AG of Australia* v. *R and Boiler Makers' Society of Australia* [1957] AC 288; [1957] 2 All ER 45, PC. **See also: ACAS; Central Arbitration Committee.**

inferior court - a court which has jurisdiction in relation to size of claim, type of claim and within a particular geographical area e.g., County Court and Magistrates Court. Arbitral tribunals are not inferior courts for the purposes of Order 52, r. 1: *AG* v. *BBC* [1981] AC 303; [1980] 3 All ER 161. **See also: High Court of Justice.**

inherent jurisdiction to refer - by virtue of the consent of the parties and where the cause is pending before the court, the court has an inherent jurisdiction to refer a matter to arbitration. This inherent jurisdiction to refer is different from Order 36 reference in that the inherent jurisdiction cannot compel the parties to arbitrate. Futhermore, while the arbitrator under Order 36 reference is an officer of the court, the arbitrator in a reference by virtue of the court's inherent jurisdiction can be anyone. **See also: Order 36 reference.**

injunction - a court order to prohibit a person from doing certain act (a prohibitory injunction) or to demand him to do certain act (a mandatory injunction). Failure to comply with such an order results in the person being guilty of contempt of court. **See also: *Mareva* injunction.**

inquisitorial procedure - a court procedure commonly practised in Continental Europe whereby the trial judge conducts inquiry into the facts, rather than the parties. The judge will lead the investigations, examine the evidence and interrogate the witnesses. Compare: **accusatorial procedure.**
　　'An arbitrator or an umpire who, in the absence of express agreement that he should do so, attempted to conduct an arbitration along inquisitorial lines might expose himself to criticism and possible removal.': *Per* Roskill LJ in *Bremer Vulkan Schiffbau und Maschinenfabrik* v. *South India Shipping Corpn Ltd* [1981] AC 909 at p. 948. **See also: adversary procedure.**

inspection of documents - see: **discovery of documents.**

inspection of property - the inspection of the subject-matter of the arbitration reference or actions in court. Unless otherwise provided in the arbitration agreement, the arbitrator has power to inspect property in respect of which an issue arises in the arbitration. The decision to inspect property is within the arbitrator's discretion. The arbitrator is under no obligation to exercise the power of inspecting the property merely because one party has requested him to do so: *Mundy* v. *Black* (1861) 30 LJ CP 193.

An arbitrator has power to make an order under section 12(1) of the Arbitration Act 1950 to allow an expert of a party to inspect the property: *Vasso (owners)* v. *Vasso (cargo owners); The Vasso* [1983] 3 All ER 211.

institutional arbitration - an arbitration conducted under the rules of a body or an institution, which may be national (e.g., London Maritime Arbitrators' Association) or international (e.g., International Chamber of Commerce) and to which the parties agreed to refer their disputes for settlement. **See also: LCIA.**

inter alia - among other things.

interim award - compare: interim judgment in an action in court. **See: interim judgment.**

Unless a contrary intention is expressed therein, every arbitration agreement shall, where such a provision is applicable to the reference, be deemed to contain a provision that the arbitrator or umpire may, if he thinks fit, make an interim award : *Section 14, Arbitration Act 1950.*

Where a final award is being set aside, the interim award will stand, if there has not been application to the court in relation to it: *A Fox & Others* v. *P G Wellfair Ltd* [1981] 2 Lloyd's Rep 514.

Where an arbitrator delivers an interim award, he can impose conditions on it: *Japan Line Ltd* v. *Aggeliki Charis Compania Maritima SA and Davies and Potter; The Angelic Grace* [1980] 1 Lloyd's Rep 288.

Interim award has the same status as final award and is enforceable in the like manner of an award: *Section 14, Arbitration Act 1950.*

interim injunction - the High Court shall have, for the purpose of and in relation to a reference, the same power of making orders in respect of interim injunctions ... as it has for the purpose of and in relation to an action or matter in the High Court: Provided that nothing ... shall be taken to prejudice any power which may be vested in an arbitrator or umpire of making order with respect to any of the matters aforesaid: *Section 12(6)(b), Arbitration Act 1950.*

interlocutory injunction - a temporary injunction usually granted pending the hearing of a case. Compare: **interim injunction. See also: interim injunction;** *Mareva* **injunction.**

interlocutory judgment - interim judgment which deals with part of the matter in dispute. Compare: **interim award.** Contrast: **final judgment.**

interlocutory matters - matters arising from the pre-trial stage of civil litigations such as injunction. **See also:** *Mareva* **injunction.**

interlocutory relief - also known as interim relief. A temporary remedy such as injunction, *Mareva* injunction etc., granted by a court at the pre-trial stage to a plaintiff. **See also:** *Mareva* **injunction.**

international arbitration - an arbitration in which the parties are nationals of different states.

International Centre for Settlement of Investment Disputes (ICSID) - under the auspices of the World Bank, the Convention on the Settlement of Investment Disputes between States and Nationals of Other States (also known as the World Bank Convention) came into force on 14 October 1966: 575 *United Nations Treaty Series* 159; (1965) 4 *International Legal Materials* 532. This Convention created the International Centre for Settlement of Investment Disputes (ICSID) with the aim, *inter alia,* to provide arbitration as a means to resolve disputes and act as 'a balanced instrument serving the interests of hosts states as well as the investors': See, A Broches, 'The Convention on the Settlement of Investment Disputes Between States and Nationals of Other States' (1972-II) *Recueil des Cours* 331. The emphasis of the ICSID is to resolve disputes arising out of investment. But currently, the ICSID has a set of Additional Facility Arbitration Rules catering for cases which are not 'investment' under the Convention but nevertheless bear similarity to investment and have special impact on the economy of the host state, e.g., major civil construction projects.

The ICSID has its headquarter in Washington D.C. but arbitrations conducted under its rules can be held elsewhere in the world.

International Chamber of Commerce - See: ICC arbitration.

International Court of Justice (ICJ) - a permanent tribunal of the United Nations, founded in 1945 as its principal judicial organ. The Court nevertheless has its seat at the Peace Palace in The Hague. The ICJ has 15 judges, who are elected by the Security Council and the General Assembly of the United Nations, each serving a tenure of fifteen years of office. Under the Statutes of the ICJ, only states may be parties to any action before the Court. The action before the Court is similar to an arbitration in that the Court has only jurisdiction to adjudicate if state parties have given their consent. **See also: World Court.**

inter-state arbitration - an arbitration where the disputants taking part in the reference are states.

Iran-United States Claims Tribunal - a tribunal set up in The Hague on 19 January 1981 'to terminate all litigations as between the government of each party and the nationals of the other, and to bring about the settlement and termination of all claims through binding arbitration'. The Tribunal adopted the UNCITRAL Arbitration Rules with modification by the parties or the Tribunal. Historically, the establishment of the Tribunal can be traced back to the serious conflicts between Iran and the United States in the late seventies and early eighties, when 52 Americans were taken hostages in Iran. A peace solution was struck by Algeria as the intermediary, whereby the Iranian Government promised to release the hostages and the United States Government agreed to defrost Iranian assets amounting to some US$12,000 million to restore the financial position of Iran and its nationals, in so far as possible, to that which existed prior to 14 November 1979.

The first case concerning the award of the Iran-United States Claims Tribunal to come before the English court is *Dallal* v. *Bank Mellat* [1986] 1 All ER 239. On the validity of such an award, the trial judge held: 'Even though the arbitration proceedings were a nullity in the municipal law where the arbitration was held, in the interests of international comity, English courts would recognise the validity of the awards of foreign arbitration tribunal whose competence was derived from international law or practice.': *Per* Hobhouse J in *Dallal* v. *Bank Mellat (ibid.)* at pp. 250 and 255.

irrevocable appointment - the authority of an arbitrator or umpire appointed by or by virtue of an arbitration agreement shall, unless a contrary intention is expressed in the agreement, be irrevocable except by leave of the High Court or a judge thereof: *Section 1, Arbitration Act 1950.*

J

J - Judge (plural: JJ) **see also: puisne judge.**

Judge - a state official appointed by the Crown to adjudicate on disputes. He can only be removed from office by a resolution of both Houses of Parliament assented to by the Crown. Most judges are barristers of at least ten years standing. But now solicitors can be appointed as judges if they have completed three years' services as recorders. Under section 4 of the Administration of Justice Act 1970, a High Court judge in the Queen's Bench Commercial Court may be appointed as an arbitrator or an umpire. (See: **Judge-arbitrator**). County Court judges are prohibited from sitting as arbitrator for a fee: *Section 6(b), County Courts Act 1956.*

Judge-arbitrator - a judge of the Commercial Court appointed as arbitrator by virtue of an arbitration agreement: *Section 1(c), Schedule 3, Administration of Justice Act 1970.*
   A judge of the Commercial Court shall not accept appointment as arbitrator unless the Lord Chief Justice has informed him that having regard to the state of business in the High Court and [in the Crown Court] he can be made available to do so: *Section 4(2), Administration of Justice Act 1970.*
   The fees payable for the services of a judge as arbitrator shall be taken in the High Court: *Section 4(3), Administration of Justice Act 1970.*

Judge-umpire - a judge of the Commercial Court appointed as umpire by virtue of an arbitration agreement: *Section 1(c), Schedule 3, Administration of Justice Act 1970.*
   Unless the Lord Chief Justice has informed the judge that he can be made available to be appointed as an umpire, no judge shall accept such appointment: *Section 4(2), Administration of Justice Act 1970.*
   The fees charged by the judge as umpire shall go to the High Court: *Section 4(3), Administration of Justice Act 1970.*

judgment - decision made by the court in respect of the matter submitted before it. The judgments of the higher courts bind the lower courts: **See:** *stare decisis;* **also: enforcement of judgment; precedent.**

judgment creditor - the person who is declared by the court to be entitled to the payment of money by the other party.

Under the Arbitration (International Investment Disputes) Act 1966, judgment creditor means the person seeking recognition or enforcement of an award : *RSC Order 73, r. 9(1).*

judgment debtor - the person ordered by the court to pay money to the other party.

Under the Arbitration (International Investment Disputes) Act 1966, judgment debtor means the other party to an award, as opposed to the party seeking recognition or enforcement of the award: *RSC Order 73, r. 9(1).*

judicial arbitration - an arbitration heard by an official referee or a judge. **See: Order 36 reference.**

judicial discretion - the power of the court to act, order, grant a remedy, or admit evidence or not as it thinks fit. Most rules of procedures are discretionary. The Court of Appeal is reluctant to review the exercise of the discretion by trial judges. Likewise the court is reluctant to review arbitrator's discretion.

judicial precedent - see: *stare decisis,* **precedent.**

judicial review - generally, the review of the decisions and judgment of the inferior courts, tribunals and administrative authorities.

Arbitral awards are subject to judicial review under certain circumstances through appeal on points of law under section 1, Arbitration Act 1979. (**See: appeal; leave to appeal**) The awards may also be reviewed by the court under sections 22, 23, and 24 of the

Arbitration Act 1950: **See: remission of award; setting aside of award.**

jurisdiction - the power of the tribunal or a court to hear and decide a case or to issue certain order; such power being defined and provided by statutes, in respect of the court.

In relation to arbitration, jurisdiction may mean one of the following:- (1) the power of the arbitral tribunal to conduct the reference; (2) the obligation of arriving at a decision in accordance with a stipulated substantive law; and (3) the obligation of arriving at a decision in accordance with a stipulated procedural law or such procedural law the tribunal is bound to follow.

These jurisdictions are provided in the arbitration agreement as well as the arbitration law of the country. **See also: arbitrator's jurisdiction; functus officio; slip rule.**

KB - King's Bench Division of the Supreme Court of Judicature. **See: Queen's Bench Division.**

L

Law Lords - Members of the House of Lords charged with judicial functions. **See: Lords of Appeal in Ordinary; House of Lords.**

law merchant - that part of international commercial and maritime practice of the merchants. The English law has adopted part of the law merchant into its common law, e.g., the law regarding the transfer of bills of lading and other negotiable instruments. 'It is neither more nor less than the usages of merchants and traders in the different departments of trade, ratified by the decisions of the Courts of law, which, upon such usages being proved before them, have adopted them as settled law with a view to the interests of trade and the public convenience, the Court proceeding herein on the well-known principle of law that, with reference to transactions in the different department of trade, Courts of law, in giving effect to the contracts and dealings of the parties, will assume that the latter have dealt with one another on the footing of any custom or usage prevailing generally in the particular department. By this process, what before was usage only, unsanctioned by legal decision, has become engrafted upon, or incorporated into, the Common Law, and may thus be said to form part of it': *Per* Cockburn, CJ in *Goodwin* v. *Robarts and Others* (1875) LR 10 Exch 337 at p. 346. The speech of Cockburn, CJ was affirmed on appeal to the House of Lords: **See:** *Goodwin* v. *Robarts* [1874-80] All ER Rep 628 HL.

In relation to arbitration, there is a move among international community to delocalise or denationalise arbitration such that international arbitration shall not be governed by municipal law of the place where the arbitration is held, but by *lex mercatoria:* **See:** *lex mercatoria.*

Law Society arbitration - See: **Solicitors Arbitration Scheme.**

LC - Lord Chancellor. **See: Lord Chancellor.**

LCA - London Court of Arbitration. Now known as London Court of International Arbitration. **See: London Court of International Arbitration.**

LCA arbitration clause (1981 Edn) - "any dispute or difference between the parties in connection with this contract (agreement) shall be referred to and determined by arbitration under the International Arbitration Rules of the London Court of Arbitration."

'Parties are also reminded that many difficulties, and much expenses, can often be saved if they expressly specify in their contract the law of the country by which it shall be governed.

If they choose English law, or if English law is for some other reason likely to apply, they may like to know that in most cases parties can, if they wish, exclude the jurisdiction of the English Courts to review an award or to determine preliminary points of law. An appropriate clause for achieving this result is:

"The parties agree to exclude any right of application or appeal to the English Courts in connexion with any question of law arising in the course of the arbitration or with respect to any award made."'

Note: The International Arbitration Rules of the LCA, 1981 Edn., which contain this arbitration clause, have been replaced by the new 1985 Edn. **(see: LCIA arbitration clause (1985) Edn.).** However, there are still a number of arbitrations left to be held under these 1981 Rules.

LCIA - London Court of International Arbitration. Formerly known as London Court of Arbitration. It is one of the oldest arbitral institutions in the world, being established in 1892. The LCIA is jointly managed by the Corporation of the City of London, the London Chamber of Commerce and Industry and the Chartered Institute of Arbitrators. The main functions of the LCIA are to organise and administer arbitrations, such as the selections and appointments of arbitrators. In this regard, it maintains a list of arbitrators. It published a new set of arbitration rules in 1985 which came into operation on 1 January 1985. These rules are closer to the UNCITRAL Model Law (see: **UNCITRAL Model Law**) in contents than any of its previous rules.

LCIA arbitration clause (1985 Edn) - "any dispute arising out of or in connection with this contract, including any question regarding its existence, validity or termination, shall be referred to and finally resolved by arbitration under the Rules of the London Court of International Arbitration, which Rules are deemed to be incorporated by reference into this clause."

'Parties are also reminded that difficulties and expense may be avoided if they expressly specify the law governing their contract. The parties may if they wish also specify the number of arbitrators, and the place and language of the arbitration. The following provisions may be suitable:

"The governing law of this contract shall be the substantive law of ...."

"The tribunal shall consist of ... (a sole or three) arbitrator(s). (In the case of a three member tribunal, the following words may be added '... two of them shall be nominated by the respective parties)'."

"The place of arbitration shall be ....(city)."

"The language of the arbitration shall be ....".

LCJ - Lord Chief Justice. **See: Lord Chief Justice.**

leapfrog procedure - the appeal directly from the High Court to the House of Lords. This is permitted under exceptional circumstances such as that the trial judge is satisfied as to the importance of the case and that the House of Lords has granted leave in this regard. **See also: appeal.**

leave - permission of the court to take some procedural steps in actions such as leave to appeal against an arbitral award under section 1 of the Arbitration Act 1979. **See: leave to appeal.**

leave to appeal - unless the consent of all the parties to the reference is obtained, an appeal against an arbitral award shall only lie to the High Court with leave of the court: *Section 1(3)(b) and section 1(5)(b),*

Arbitration Act 1979. The High Court shall not grant leave under section 1(3)(b) unless it considers that, having regard to all the circumstances, the determination of the question of law concerned could substantially affect the rights of one or more of the parties to the arbitration agreement; and the court may make any leave which it gives conditional upon the applicant complying with such conditions as it considers appropriate: *Section 1(4), Arbitration Act 1979.* In any case where an award is made without any reason being given, the High Court shall not grant leave to appeal unless it is satisfied - (a) that before the award was made one of the parties to the reference gave notice to the arbitrator or umpire concerned that a reasoned award would be required; or (b) that there is some special reason why such a notice was not given: *Section 1(6), Arbitration Act 1979.* The High Court shall not, under section 1(3)(b) [of the Arbitration Act 1979], grant leave to appeal with respect to a question of law arising out of an award, (b) the High Court shall not, under section 1(5)(b) [of the Arbitration Act 1979], grant leave to make application with respect to an award, and (c) no application may be made under section 2(1)(a) [of the Arbitration Act 1979], with respect to a question of law, if the parties to the reference in question have entered into an agreement in writing (in this section referred to as an "exclusion agreement") which excludes the right of appeal under section 1[of the Arbitration Act 1979] in relation to that award or, in a case falling within paragraph 3(1)(c), in relation to an award to which the determination of the question of law is material: *Section 3(1), Arbitration Act 1979.* **(See also: exclusion agreement;** *Nema* **Guidelines, the.)**

Unless the High Court gives leave, no appeal shall lie to the Court of Appeal from a decision of the High Court - (a) to grant or refuse leave under section 1(3)(b) or section 1(5)(b) of the Arbitration Act 1979; or (b) to make or not to make an order under section 1(5) of the Arbitration Act 1979: *Section 1(6A), Arbitration Act 1979.*

No appeal shall lie to the Court of Appeal from a decision of the High Court on an appeal unless - (a) the High Court or the Court of Appeal gives leave; and (b) it is certified by the High Court that the question of law to which its decision relates either is one of general public importance or is one which for some other special reason should be considered by the Court of Appeal: *Section 1(7), Arbitration Act 1979.*

Applications for leave to appeal under section 1(2) of the Arbitration Act 1979 or under section 1(5) of that Act, including any application for leave, are to be made to a Judge in Chambers: *S.I. 1983 No. 1181.*

Where application for leave to appeal is made, it will be heard at a separate hearing; rather than together with the appeal, if any: *Tor Line AB* v. *Alltrans Group of Canada Ltd* [1982] 1 Lloyd's Rep 617 at pp. 626-627.

legal arbitration - the reference of which the arbitrator is bound to resolve the dispute in question in the same manner as a judge, as distinct from mere valuation or certification or pay or industrial arbitration. The presence of an arbitration agreement and of dispute, the tendering of evidence, the examination of witnesses and the rendering of final and binding awards are the characteristics of a legal arbitration. Nevertheless, the arbitrator of a legal arbitration need not be a legally qualified person; nor the advocates of the parties be legally qualified persons such as barristers or solicitors. **See also: advocates.**

legal arbitrator - an arbitrator who is also a legal practitioner or a legally qualified person.

legal misconduct - the admission of inadmissible evidence: *Agroexport Enterprise d'Etat pour le Commerce Exterieur* v. *NV Goorden Import Cy SA* [1956] 1 Lloyd's Rep 319; *Walford Baker & Co* v. *Macfie & Sons* (1915) 84 LJ KB 2221. **See also: misconduct; technical misconduct.**

legal proceedings - under the Civil Evidence Act 1968, legal proceedings include arbitrations or references whether under an enactment or not: *Section 18(2), Civil Evidence Act 1968.* **See also: proceedings; reference.**

legal professional privilege - (1) the right to withhold communications between lawyers and their clients and also between lawyers and the third parties with a view to advising their clients; and (2) the right to withhold communications marked 'without prejudice' in the course of litigation.

lex arbitri - the law of arbitration reference. It may be different from the law of the place where arbitration is held. **See also: *lex loci arbitri*.**

lex domicilii - law of a country of a person's domicile.

lex fori - the law of the forum or court in which a case is tried. More particularly the law relating to procedure or the formalities in force (adjective law) in a given place. **See also: adjective law.**

lex loci arbitri - the arbitration law of the place where the reference is being conducted and held.

lex loci contractus - the law of the place where a contract is made.

lex loci solutionis - the law of the place of performance or payment.

lex mercatoria - a body of merchant-made rules which has developed from trade customs and usages in international trade. A law, a set of rules which derives from the usages accumulated in the field covered by the contract recognised under the general principles of national jurisdical systems and common to all nations: *re Arbitration between Texaco Overseas Petroleum Company and California Asiatic Oil Company AND the Government of the Libyan Arab Republic*, 53 *International Law Reports* 389 at p. 447. There is a growing trend in international commercial arbitration to detach arbitrations from the applications of municipal law and to subject the arbitration to *lex mercatoria*. **See also: law merchant.**

lex situs - law of the place where the property is held.

LIAT - The London International Arbitration Trust, **see: London International Arbitration Trust, The**

liberty to apply - a common clause in an Order for Directions which specifies that the parties may apply to the arbitrator, if necessary, in the actual hearing, for matters not listed in the Order for Directions, e.g., for extension of time, for permission to amend pleadings etc. **See also: Order for Directions.**

liquidated damages - see **damages.**

lis - a suit or action, where there is an issue between parties in dispute.

lis alibi pendens - a suit pending elsewhere (Latin). If there is a litigation between the same parties in respect of the same dispute, the court may grant a stay of proceeding. If there is an arbitration reference pending, the proceedings on the same disputes concerning the same parties may be stayed by the court: *Section 4, Arbitration Act 1950.*

litigants - parties which contest in law by pursuing an action in court. Compare: **claimants** and **respondents** in arbitration. **See also: plaintiff;   defendant.**

litigation - a term describing legal actions in court.

live dispute - existing dispute. An arbitrator has no jurisdiction to act if the dispute has ceased to be a live dispute before he is appointed.

LJ - Lord Justice. (Plural, LJJ). **See: Lord Justice of Appeal.**

Lloyd's Form Arbitration - a type of arbitration held under Lloyd's Form of Salvage Agreement relating to salvage reward. The signing of the Lloyd's Form constitutes the consent of the parties to the jurisdiction of the arbitrators to determine the amount of the salvage award. The procedure of the arbitration are similar to other types of arbitration except that there is no pleading and no particular unless in exceptional circumstances where negligence of the salvors is being alleged. Since it is the normal practice of this type of arbitration that the salvaged values are agreed by the solicitors of both parties before the arbitration, the actual proceeding rarely last longer than one or two days.

It is usual for salvors in accordance with the Form to notify the Committee of Lloyds that they require the shipowners to put up security to cover costs, expenses and interest. However, where security is given, any claim for arbitrations must be made within 42 days from the date of completion of such security. The claim of Lloyd's Form Arbitration is a claim within the meaning of section 27 of the Arbitration Act 1950: *Sioux Inc* v. *China Salvage Co, Kwangchow Branch and another; The American Sioux* [1980] 3 All ER 154 CA.

LMAA - London Maritime Arbitrators' Association. **See: London Maritime Arbitrators' Association.**

LMAA arbitration - arbitration conducted by the members of the LMAA. But such an arbitration is by no means an administered arbitration **(see: administered arbitration)** for the LMAA does not directly supervise or administer the proceedings. The LMAA maintains a panel of arbitrators who are also 'commercial men'. **(See: commercial men).** It also published the 'LMAA Terms (1984)' to govern the relationship of the parties and the proceedings generally. However, the acceptance of these Terms is optional, since the Committee of the LMAA only recommends that LMAA members accepting appointment as arbitrators should subject their appointments to the LMAA Terms. Hence, LMAA arbitrations are subject to Arbitration Acts 1950-1979, case-law and LMAA Terms, if agreed.

A characteristic of the LMAA arbitrations is that awards rendered by the LMAA arbitrators customarily contain reasons. These reasons are issued as a matter of course, frequently on LMAA arbitrators' own initiative. However, unlike other maritime arbitral institutions in the world, e.g., the Society of Maritime Arbitrators Inc. in New York, the awards of the LMAA arbitrators are confidential and not published. The LMAA arbitrators conduct the bulk of maritime arbitrations held in London.

LMAA arbitration clause - 'Any dispute arising out of, or in connection with, this contract or any Bill of Lading issued thereunder shall be referred to a sole arbitrator in London to be appointed by the parties. If the parties do not appoint a sole arbitrator, then each party shall appoint an arbitrator, and the arbitrators, if unable to agree on their Award, shall appoint an Umpire. If a party fails to appoint an arbitrator either originally or by way of substitution within 14 days of being called on to do so, the other party may, in order to complete the Arbitration Tribunal, apply to the President of the London Maritime Arbitrators' Association, c/o The Baltic Exchange, St. Mary Axe, London EC3A 8BU (with a copy to the party who has failed to appoint an arbitrator) for the appointment of an arbitrator on behalf of that party. The Award of the sole arbitrator, two arbitrators or the Umpire (as the case may be) shall be final and binding on the parties.

This contract and all arbitration proceedings shall be governed by English law.'

LMAA exclusion clause - 'If and insofar as English law applies to the arbitration hereby agreed, the parties further agree to exclude any right of application or appeal to the English Courts in connection with any question of law arising in the course of the reference or out of the Award.'

locus standi - a place to stand (Latin). The right to commence an action or to defend in court, or to commence or defend an arbitration.

London Court of International Arbitration - See: LCIA.

London arbitration clause - an arbitration clause which provides for arbitration reference to be held in London. The procedure and other similar matters are governed by English law and practice.

London International Arbitration Trust, The (LIAT) - an umbrella organisation to several arbitral institutions in the City of London to promote, support and co-ordinate arbitrations in London. However, it is not, *per se,* involved in the reference. Officially set up on 26 July 1983, the LIAT encourages international business community to hold arbitrations in London through its publications,

Arbitration in London, and its advisory service manned by its International Arbitration Counsellor.

London Maritime Arbitrators' Association - an arbitral institution based in the Baltic Exchange in the City of London, to provide services to the maritime industry. It was formed in 1961 and has 43 members (1985 figures). These members elect a committee of seven annually, which committee, in turn, elects a President among them. It also has a group of Supporting Members totalling 360 in 1985 who are lawyers, brokers, owners, bankers and P&I Club people. This category of members are interested and concerned with the work of the LMAA but do not aspire to be ordinary members of the LMAA, or would not qualify as such. Most of the maritime arbitrations held in London are conducted under the auspices of the LMAA. **See also: LMAA arbitration; LMAA arbitration clause.**

Lord Advocate - the equivalent of English Attorney-General in Scotland. Though he is not always a Member of Parliament, the office of the Lord Advocate is a political appointment made by the government of the day.

Lord Chancellor - the head of the judiciary, the Speaker of the House of Lords and a government minister normally of Cabinet rank. He is a rare person in the British Constitutional structure who possesses all three judicial, executive and legislative functions. In respect of his judicial functions, he sits in the House of Lords (though not normally). He makes judicial appointments, e.g., appointing magistrates, and is in charge of the functioning of the judiciary. In respect of his legislative functions, he sits in the House of Lords as its Speaker and is free to vacate his seat and participate in debates. His appointment is made by the Crown on the advice of the Prime Minister of the day.

Lord Chief Justice (LCJ) - the second highest judicial office after the Lord Chancellor. He is the chief judge of the Queen's Bench Division of the High Court of Justice, an *ex officio* member of the Court of Appeal and also the President of the Criminal Division of the

Court of Appeal. He is appointed from amongst the Lord Justices of Appeal (LJJ) and the Lords of Appeal in Ordinary (Law Lords).

Lord Justice of Appeal (LJ) - a judge of the Court of Appeal and a Member of the Privy Council. The Lord Justices (LJJ) are normally appointed by the Crown on the advice of the Prime Minister from amongst the puisne judges of the High Court, although in principle, it is possible for a barrister of at least 15 years' standing to be appointed as a LJ.

Lords of Appeal in Ordinary - Law Lords. There are eleven in number and they are members of the House of Lords charged with judicial functions, sitting as a final court of appeal. They are appointed like peerages by the Crown on the advice of the Prime Minister under the Appellate Jurisdiction Act 1876 from amongst holders of high judicial office or practising barristers of at least 15 years' standing. They normally sit in a court of five.

***Lysland* Principle, the** - the principle enunciated by Lord Denning in *Halfdan Grieg & Co A/S* v. *Sterling Coal & Navigation Corpn & another; The Lysland* [1973] 2 WLR 904 regarding the arbitrator's exercise of his discretion to state a case for the determination of the court.

'The point of law should be real and substantial and such as to be open to serious argument and appropriate for decision by a court of law ... as distinct from a point which is dependent on the special expertise of the arbitrator ... .

The point of law should be clear cut and capable of being accurately stated as a point of law - as distinct from the dressing up of a matter of fact as if it were a point of law.

The point of law should be of such importance that the resolution of it is necessary for the proper determination of the case - as distinct from a side issue of little importance ... .'

M

manifest disregard of English law - an arbitrator may be found to arrive at his award with manifest disregard of law, if the award has not been rendered in accordance with the principles of English law. This is to be distinguished from an award which contains error of law. Where an award is the result of manifest disregard of law, the award may be set aside. But an award which contains error of law is not susceptible to challenge, for the High Court shall not have jurisdiction to set aside or remit an award on the ground of errors of law on the face of the award: *Section 1(1), Arbitration Act 1979.* **See: (error of law).** Examples of manifest disregard of English law are: (a) to conduct an arbitration in inquisitorial procedure (**see: inquisitorial procedure**) in the absence of express agreement by the parties; and (b) to deliver an award by *ex aequo et bono,* in the absence of express agreement by the parties etc. (**See:** *ex aequo et bono).*

Mareva **injunction** - the interlocutory relief named after *Mareva Compania SA* v. *International Bulk Carriers* [1975] 2 Lloyd's Rep 509, originally to prevent a defendant from removing assets from the jurisdiction so that enforcement of judgment is impossible. Now, the order restrains the defendant of all disposals of assets: *Z Ltd* v. *A-Z* [1982] 1 Lloyd's Rep 240. In relation to arbitration clause, the prohibition of legal proceedings contained therein includes *Mareva* injunction: *Montovani* v. *Carapelli SpA* [1980] 1 Lloyd's Rep 375. **See:** *Scott* **v.** *Avery* **Clause.**

In relation to arbitration, since *Mareva* injunction is essentially an interim relief, parties may apply to the High Court for an order to grant *Mareva* injunction under section 12(6)(h) of the Arbitration Act 1950, or to secure amount in dispute in the reference under section 12(6)(f) of the Arbitration Act 1950. '... it appears to me that both section 12(6)(f) and (h) cover the granting of a *Mareva* injunction, and so give the court the same power to grant such an injunction for the purpose of and in relation to an arbitration as it has for the purpose of and in relation to an action or matter in the court. ... and to do so subject to a term providing for the arbitration to be commenced within a specified time, together with such other terms, if any, as it thinks fit.': *Per* Brandon J in *The Rena K* [1978] 1 Lloyd's Rep 545 at pp. 561 - 562; [1979] QB 377 at p. 408. Note also the power of the High Court in granting injunction, whether interlocutory or final, under section 37 of the Supreme Court Act 1981.

maritime arbitration - a specialised arbitration usually held by maritime arbitrators' associations concerning maritime transactions. Almost all maritime arbitrations are conducted by the London Maritime Arbitrators' Association, the New York Society of Maritime Arbitrators Inc., the Tokyo Maritime Arbitrators' Association and the Maritime Arbitration Commission in China and the International Court of Arbitration for Marine and Inland Navigation at Gdynia.

The nature of a maritime arbitration held in London is well-described by Donaldson J (as he then was) in *The Myron* [1969] 1 Lloyd's Rep 411 at p. 415: 'Each party appoints one arbitrator, and the arbitrators so appointed are empowered to appoint an umpire. In order to avoid expense an umpire is not normally appointed unless it is apparent that the arbitrators are unlikely to be able to agree upon an award.

The arbitrators are appointed to perform a judicial function unless and until they disagree and the umpire enters upon the reference. Thereafter they can and do act as advocates for the parties who appointed them. Until that point is reached, and it is only in a minority of cases that it is reached, neither arbitrator has any special relationship with the party which appointed him and each arbitrator is under the same duty of fairness, openness and impartiality to both parties.

In a few cases Counsel and solicitors are retained and the proceedings take on a more formal character which is akin to the procedure in a Court of law. In the majority of cases informality is the keynote and the recognized channel by which a party communicates with the arbitrators is via the arbitrator whom he has appointed. This in no sense makes that arbitrator the agent or delegate of the party who appointed him. Any evidence or submissions so received by an arbitrator must be, and I hope always is, communicated to the other arbitrator at once or at the arbitrators' next meeting.

In most cases neither party wishes to have the opportunity of submitting oral evidence or argument to the arbitrators and the matter is dealt with by the arbitrators at a private meeting or meetings at which they consider all the material which has been placed before them by either party.

...In the context of a London shipping arbitration, parties impliedly agree to the customary procedure subject only to the qualification that they can, on giving due notice, require matters to be handled with strict formality and, in particular, can require an oral hearing. That this procedure works well and is very widely welcomed by the international shipping community is a matter of common knowledge ...'

See generally: **LMAA arbitration.**

mandamus - a writ issued by a higher court to a lower court.

Masters - permanent officers of the court in charge of administration who are in particular, responsible for those interlocutory pre-trial matters. The parties have no right to choose a particular Master to hear their case.

Master of the Rolls (MR) - an ancient office originally held by the keeper of the public records. Later, he became the assistant to the Lord Chancellor and sat in his own court, the *Rolls Court.* Now the MR is the president of the Civil Division of the Court of Appeal. He also admits solicitors to practice.

Masters of the Supreme Court - judicial officers of the Queen's Bench and Chancery Divisions of the High Court. Their main duties are to supervise interlocutory proceedings and especially in the Chancery Division to take accounts.

misconduct - all allegations of misconduct assert that the arbitrator has acted in breach of duty; and most involve the contention that the arbitrator has failed to act fairly or at least to appear to act fairly.

'Such a mishandling of the arbitrations as is likely to amount to some substantial miscarriage of justice.' *Per* Atkin J in *Williams* v. *Wallis & Cox* [1914] 2 KB 478 at p. 485.

'Misconduct is an unfortunate term of art used to denote procedural unfairness, almost always involving no reflection on the competence or integrity of the arbitrator.' *Per* Bingham J in *Bulk Oil (ZUG) AG* v. *Sun International Ltd and Sun Oil Trading Co (No. 2)* [1984] 1 Lloyd's Rep 531 at p. 533; 'Misconduct ... gives the impression that some impropriety or breach of professional conduct or lack of integrity or incompetence is involved.' *Per* Bingham J in *Zermalt Holdings SA* v. *Nu-Life Upholstery Repairs Ltd* (1985) 275 Estates Gazette 1134 at p. 1137.

To err in law or in fact is not misconduct: *Port Sudan Cotton Co* v. *Govindaswamy Chettiar & Sons* [1977] 1 Lloyd's Rep 166.

To impose condition in an interim award is not misconduct: *Japan Line Ltd* v. *Aggeliki Charis Compania Maritima SA and Davies and Porter; The Angelic Grace* [1980] 1 Lloyd's Rep 288.

The fact that there is no hearing in an arbitration reference does not make the arbitrator guilty of misconduct: *Star International Hong Kong (UK) Ltd* v. *Bergbau-Handel GmbH* [1966] 2 Lloyd's Rep 16.

To be assisted by a solicitor (even of one of the parties) in preparation of the award, after the conclusion is reached, is not misconduct: *Bunten & Lancaster (Produce) Ltd* v. *Kiril Mischeff Ltd* [1964] 1 Lloyd's Rep 386.

The fact that the arbitrators do not require the presence of the parties in a reference is not misconduct, unless the parties desire to be heard and shown their intention in this regard: *A A Amram Ltd* v. *Bremer Co Ltd* [1966] 1 Lloyd's Rep 494.

To refuse to accept evidence or to award costs or to delay his award is not misconduct: *Lewis Emanuel & Son Ltd* v. *Sammut* [1959] 2 Lloyd's Rep 629.

Where parties choose to have informal arbitration and unreasoned award, the arbitrator's decision on an unpleaded issue does not make him guilty of misconduct: *Atlantic Lines and Navigation Co Inc* v. *Italmare SpA; The Apollon* [1985] 1 Lloyd's Rep 597.

Inconsistency between one part of an award and another cannot constitute evidence of misconduct on the part of the arbitrator: *Moran* v. *Lloyd's* [1983] 2 All ER 200.

To refuse adjournment of hearing is not misconduct: *The Sanko Steamship Co Ltd* v. *The Shipping Corpn of India and Selwyn and Clark; The Jhansi Ki Rani* [1980] 2 Lloyd's Rep 569.

Arbitrator's failure to give clear warning on *ex parte* reference is misconduct: *The Myron (Owners)* v. *Tradax Export SA* [1969] 1 Lloyd's Rep 411. But note the power of the arbitrator or umpire to proceed with an *ex parte* reference in like manner as a judge without giving warning to the parties under section 5(2) of the Arbitration Act 1979.

It is misconduct for the arbitrator to act unfairly and without impartiality between the parties: *re An Arbitration between the owners of steamship Catalina and others and the owners of motor vessel Norma* (1938) 61 Ll LR 360.

It can be misconduct to fail in important respects to show the elementary skill of an arbitrator: *Pratt* v. *Swanmore Builders Ltd & Baker* [1980] 2 Lloyd's Rep 504.

To inspect property in question with only one party amounts to misconduct: *In the Matter of an arbitration between Brien and Brien* [1910] 2 IR 84.

Excessive charging of fees by the arbitrator may be misconduct: *re An Arbitration between Prebble and Robinson and another* [1892] 2 QB 602; *Appleton* v. *Norwich Union Fire Insurance Society Ltd* (1922) 13 Ll LR 345.

See also: **moral misconduct; legal misconduct; technical misconduct.**

moral misconduct - dishonesty or breach of business morality upon the part of the arbitrator. Normally, the term denotes misconduct of the arbitrator as the result of being bias or having interest in the reference such that he acts unfairly and without impartiality between the parties. See: **misconduct; legal misconduct; technical misconduct; bias.**

MR - Master of the Rolls. See: **Master of the Rolls.**

multiple arbitration - an arbitration which involves more than two parties to the arbitration agreement, such as a third party. For example, a building owner may claim arbitration against the contractor (with whom he has an arbitration agreement) and the architect of the contractor (with whom he has no arbitration agreement, but may have arbitration agreement with the contractor). See also the case of *Northern Regional Health Authority* v. *Derek Crouch Construction Co Ltd* [1984] 2 All ER 175 CA. **See also: string arbitration.**

mutatis mutandis - after making the necessary changes.

mutual obligations in arbitration - '... parties to the reference, and all persons claiming through them respectively, shall, subject to any legal objection, submit to be examined by the arbitrator or umpire, on oath or affirmation, in relation to the matters in dispute, and shall, subject as aforesaid, produce before the arbitrator or umpire all documents within their possession or power respectively which may be required or called for, and do all other things which during the proceedings on the reference the arbitrator or umpire may require': *Section 12(1) of the Arbitration Act 1950.* '... both claimant and respondent may carry out voluntarily some or all of the preliminary steps needed to prepare the matter for the hearing by the arbitrator, and do so without seeking and obtaining prior direction from him; but, if what is done voluntarily by way of preparation is done so tardily that it threatens to delay the hearing to a date when there will be a substantial risk that justice cannot be done, it is in my view a necessary implication from their having agreed that the arbitrator shall resolve their dispute that both parties, respondent as well as claimant, are under a mutual obligation to one another to join in applying to the arbitrator for appropriate directions to put an end to the delay.' *Per* Lord Diplock in *Bremer Vulkan Schiffbau und Maschinenfabrik* v. *South India Shipping Corpn* [1981] 1 All ER 289 at p. 301.

N

NAEGA - North American Export Grain Association Inc.

National Small Claims Arbitration Service - a service provided by the Chartered Institute of Arbitrators offering an inexpensive and informal method of resolving disputes arising between subscribers to the National Small Claims Arbitration service and their customers. This service is governed by the National Small Claims Arbitration Service Rules of the Chartered Institute of Arbitrators (1985/86 Edition). Under Rule 5, an arbitration is possible only if both parties submit a joint application for arbitration on the prescribed application form.

The arbitration, which will generally be on documents only, will be governed by such law as agreed by the parties, or absent such agreement, as the arbitrator may direct: *Rules 7 and 13(i)*.

Any dissatisfied arbitrant may appeal against the decision of the arbitrator, subject to the provisions of the relevant Arbitration Acts currently in force.

natural justice - rules of fair play: (a) Rules against bias - *nemo judex in causa sua* (or in *propria causa*) (Latin: no man may be a judge in his own cause); (b) Rules to hear the other side - *audi alteram partem*. Thus, this is one of the foundations of the adversarial system of justice : that a party must be given the opportunity of answering the case against him. **(See also: adversary procedure).**

An arbitrator will be removed for misconduct if he contravenes natural justice in his conducting of the arbitration reference: *A Fox* v. *P G Wellfair Ltd; P Fisher* v. *P G Wellfair Ltd* [1981] 2 Lloyd's Rep 514 CA. **See also: expert knowledge of the arbitrator.**

negotiable instrument - a document which obliges a party to pay a sum of money. Since it is transferable by the holder to the transferee, it is 'negotiable'. Examples of negotiable instruments are bills of lading and bills of exchange including: cheques, promissory notes, dividend, warrants, share warrants, interest warrants, etc.   **See: Bill of Lading.**

Nema **Guidelines, the** - guidelines on the court's discretion in granting leave to appeal under section 1 of the Arbitration Act 1979 as delivered by the House of Lords in *Pioneer Shipping Ltd and others*   v. *BTP Tioxide Ltd; The Nema* [1981] 2 All ER 1030 HL.

'Where ... the question of law involved is the construction of a one-off clause the application of which to the particular facts of the case is in issue in the arbitration, leave should not normally be given unless it is apparent to the judge, on a mere perusal of the reasoned award itself without the benefit of adversarial argument, that the meaning ascribed to the clause by the arbitrator is obviously wrong; but if on such perusal it appears to the judge that it is possible that argument might persuade him, despite impression to the contrary, that the arbitrator might be right, he should not grant leave; the parties should be left to accept, for better or for worse, the decision of the tribunal that they had chosen to decide the matter in the first instance. ... rather less strict criteria are in my view appropriate where questions of construction of contracts in standard terms are concerned. That there should be as high a degree of legal certainty as it is practicable to obtain as to how such terms apply on the occurrence of events of a kind that it is not unlikely may reproduce themselves in similar transactions between other parties engaged in the same trade is a public interest that is recognised by the 1979 Act, particularly in section 4. So, if the decision of the question of construction in the circumstances of the particular case would add significantly to the clarity and certainty of English commercial law it would be proper to give leave in a case sufficiently substantial to escape the ban imposed by the first part of section 1(4), bearing in mind always that a superabundance of citable judicial decisions arising out of slightly different facts is calculated to hinder rather than to promote clarity in settled principles of commercial law. But leave should not be given, even in such a case, unless the judge considered that a strong *prima facie* case had been made out that the arbitrator had been wrong in his construction; and when the events to which the standard clause fell to be applied in the particular arbitration were themselves one-off events stricter criteria should be applied on the same lines as those that I have suggested as appropriate to one-off clauses.

In deciding how to exercise his discretion whether to give leave to appeal under section 1(2) what the judge should normally ask himself in this type of arbitration, particularly where the events relied on are one-off events, is not whether he agrees with the decision reached by the arbitrator, but: does it appear on perusal of the award either that the arbitrator misdirect himself in law or that his decision was such that no reasonable arbitrator could reach? While this should, in my view, be the normal practice, there may be cases where the events relied on as amounting to frustration are not one-off events affecting only the transaction between the particular parties to the arbitration but events of a general character that affect similar transactions between many other persons engaged in the same kind of commercial activity; the closing of the Suez Canal, the United States soya-bean embargo, the war between Iraq and Iran, are instances within the last two decades that spring to mind. Where such is the case it is in the interests of legal certainty that there should be some uniformity in the decisions of arbitrators as to the effect, frustrating or otherwise, of such an event on similar transactions, in order that other traders may be sufficiently certain where they stand as to be able to close their own transactions without recourse to arbitration. In such a case, unless there were prospects of an appeal being brought by consent of all the parties as a test case under section 1(3)(a), it might be a proper exercise of the judge's discretion to give leave to appeal in order to express a conclusion as to the frustrating effect of the event that would afford guidance binding on the arbitrators in other arbitrations arising out of the same event, if the judge thought that in the particular case in which leave to appeal was sought the conclusion reached by the arbitrator, although not deserving to be stigmatised as one which no reasonable person could have reached, was, in the judge's view, not right ... .'

'The speeches in *The Nema* were intended to provide guidelines rather than to remove the discretion granted to the judge hearing the application and guidelines by definition permitted exceptions, albeit great care must be exercised to ensure that the exceptions do not become so numerous as to blur the edges of the guidelines or even render them invisible.' *Per* Sir John Donaldson MR in *Antaios Cia Naviera SA* v. *Salen Rederierna AB; The Antaios* [1983] 3 All ER 777 at p. 780.

The *Nema Guidelines* may not cater for a case touching on EEC law: *Bulk Oil AG* v. *Sun International Ltd* [1984] 1 All ER 386 CA.

New York Convention, 1958 - the Convention on the Recognition and Enforcement of Foreign Arbitral Awards adopted by the United Nations Conference on International Commerical Arbitration, done at New York, on 10 June 1958. The texts, which are in all five United Nations official languages, viz, Chinese, English, French, Russian and Spanish, are printed in the United Nations Treaty Series (1950) 330. All texts in the official languages are equally authentic: *Article XVI*.

The New York Convention has been given effect in England by virtue of the enactment of the Arbitration Act 1975. **See: Arbitration Act 1975.**

NOFOTA - Netherlands Oils, Fats and Oilseeds Trade Association.

O

oath administering - if the arbitrator so requires, the parties and their witnesses shall be examined on oath or affirmation in a reference: *Section 12(1) & (2) of the Arbitration Act 1950.* Section 12(3) of the 1950 Act empowers the arbitrator to administer the oaths, unless a contrary intention is expressed in the arbitration agreement. However, it is unusual for an arbitrator to administer oath in a commercial arbitration. **See also: affirmation.**

obiter - by the way, cursorily.

obiter dictum - an opinion or remark expressed by a judge in the course of his judgment as an incidental statement. Thus, it is not binding as a precedent. Compare: *ratio decidendi.*

offers to settle - parties to an arbitration reference may make offers to settle their disputes. These offers can be made either before the commencement of or during the reference. Where parties offer to settle before the reference, the exercise is akin to conciliation. Where offers are made during the reference, they are of three kinds viz: open offer, sealed offer and 'without prejudice' offer. The making of an offer during a reference, apart from having an intention to settle the disputes, can on many occasions, be a tactical move to protect the offeror against costs. This is especially so in the case where the offer exceeds the award. But for the offeree's acceptance of the offer and *ex hypothesi* , the continuation of the reference would be unnecessary and consequently, the offeree should be made to bear the costs incurred after the date of the offer. **See: open offer; sealed offer; 'without prejudice' offer.**

Official Referees - the permanent officers of the court who hear Order 36 reference, which is a form of arbitration, in rotation. Thus the parties have no right to choose any particular Referee as their arbitrator. He can sit singly in the reference or with assessors. In conducting the reference, he has the same jurisdiction, power and duties as a judge. Thus, the reference before him will be conducted in the like manner as proceedings before a judge. His award carries the same force as a judgment of the court and is enforced by execution in the same manner as a judgment. He can also commit parties for contempt of court, if such instance arises.

In spite of the above, parties may by agreement refer their disputes to a reference by an Official Referee. Section 11 of the Arbitration Act 1950, provides: 'where an arbitration agreement provides that the reference shall be to an official referee, any official referee to whom application is made shall, subject to any order of the High Court or a judge thereof as to transfer or otherwise, hear and determine the matters agreed to be referred.'

See also: Order 36 Reference.

one-off case - 'A case may be a "one-off" case either because the issue turns on a clause designed by the parties to the contract to suit their own special circumstances, being a clause unlikely to be used by any other parties, or because the facts which give rise to the dispute are not unusual and so obviously peculiar to the situation of the two parties who are litigating that, again, it is a factual position in which other parties are unlikely to find themselves. By contrast it is clear that a case is not to be regarded as "one-off" if it is dealing with a standard clause in a contract because then the proper construction of that clause is a question of interest to all users. It is equally plain that a case may take itself out of the "one-off" category, at any rate to some extent, if it is a factual situation which involves many people in a commercial context. The closure of the Suez Canal is one example; the war between India and Pakistan is another; the war between Iran and Iraq is another, ...' *Per* Bingham J in *Phoenix Shipping Corpn* v. *Apex Shipping Corpn; The Apex* [1982] 1 Lloyd's Rep 476 at p. 479.

A standard form contract containing a typewritten additional clause is not a 'one-off' contract: *Phoenix Shipping Corpn* v. *Apex Shipping Corpn; The Apex (ibid.)*.

In general, where an arbitration is a 'one-off' case, the court will normally refuse to give leave to appeal unless it is apparent to the judge that the decision of the arbitrator is obviously wrong: *Pioneer Shipping*

Ltd and others v. *BTP Tioxide Ltd; The Nema* [1982] 2 All ER 1030, HL.

See: *Nema* **Guidelines, the; leave to appeal.**

open offer - either party to an arbitration reference may make an open offer to settle to the other. This is done by handing a letter stating the offer to the arbitrator. Compare, the payment into court in an action.

'An open offer ... is one to which either party can refer at any stage of the proceedings. In an appropriate case, it may influence the arbitrator both in his decision on the matters in dispute and on the order as to costs' *Per* Donaldson J in *Tramountana Armadora SA* v. *Atlantic Shipping Co SA* [1978] 2 All ER870 at p. 876.

'An open offer, ... carries no interest for however long it remains in existence, unless it expressly says so. And interest continues to accrue to the offeror on the funds which he has in hand and will use to implement the offer if it is accepted ...' *Per* Staughton J in *La Pintada Compania Navegacion SA* v. *The President of India; The La Pintada* [1983] 1 Lloyd's Rep 37 at p. 42.

opinion evidence - the opinion of the expert witness on any matter within his expertise which if asked, can be admissible as evidence. Generally, an opinion evidence of a non-expert witness is inadmissible, subject to some exceptions.

oral evidence - statements made verbally by witness in a proceeding.

oral hearing - the presentation of case and oral argument in a trial or a reference. An arbitration reference need not necessarily have an oral hearing if the parties so desire, or if the amount in dispute is small. **(See: consumer arbitration).** The fact that there is no hearing in an arbitration reference does not make the arbitrator guilty of misconduct: *Star International Hong Kong (UK) Ltd* v. *Bergbau-Handel GmbH* [1966] 2 Lloyd's Rep 16.

Order 36 Reference - the High Court has power to refer a matter to arbitration under RSC Order 36, made under section 15 of the Administration of Justice Act 1956. The parties have no power to appoint the arbitrator in this reference which is normally presided by an Official Referee (see: **Official Referee**). A Master of the Supreme Court or a Special Referee (see: **Special Referee**) may sit as the arbitrator. The references under Order 36 are for trial (Rule 1) and for inquiry and report (Rule 2). Order 36 is actually the replacement of sections 88 and 89 of the Judicature Act 1925. Compare: **inherent jurisdiction to refer.**

Order for Directions - an Order given by the arbitrator to the parties after the preliminary meeting directing them on matters of procedures and time-table of the various stages of the arbitration reference. Sometimes the Order for Directions may be agreed by the parties through correspondence and a copy of the draft is forwarded to the arbitrator for his approval. **See also: preliminary meeting; liberty to apply.**

ordinary arbitration - in Scotland, ordinary arbitration is the term used when the parties choose arbitration as a means to settle their dispute after it has arisen.

original arbitrator - an arbitrator appointed by or at the request of a party as its nominee, particularly in an LMAA arbitration. (See: **LMAA arbitration**). In appointing an umpire or a third arbitrator, the original arbitrators shall be deemed to be acting as the agents of the parties. **See also: party-appointed arbitrators.**

original evidence - evidence of a statement made by a person who is not a testifying witness. The purpose of such evidence is to prove the existence of the statement rather than to prove the substance of the statement, i.e., the truth of the statement.

Originating Summons - an originating process in the High Court to determine an issue of law or the interpretation of document by means of submitting affidavit as evidence. Apart from providing sufficient particulars to identify the cause of action, the originating summons must include statement of the question to enable the court to determine, or statement of remedy to which the court can declare.

Matters in relation to Arbitration Acts 1950-1979, which need not be commenced by originating motion, e.g., the application for the court to appoint an arbitrator under section 10 of the Arbitration Act 1950 shall be commenced by originating summons made in the prescribed Form 10 of Appendix A in Part 2 of the Supreme Court Practice: *RSC Order 73, r. 3(3)*. **See also: Expedited Form.**

ouster of jurisdiction - the exclusion of judicial proceedings by agreement of the parties. In relation to arbitration, the agreement to preclude the jurisdiction of the court to review an arbitration award. **See: exclusion agreement; waiver.**

Oversman - the terms used in Scots law for an umpire.

P

P & I Clubs - the Protection and Indemnity Clubs. **See: Protection and Indemnity Clubs.**

paramount clause - a clause which states that the Hague Rules are to apply to carriage under a bill of lading from any port in Great Britain or Northern Ireland to any port and also to carriage between any state which have adopted the Hague Rules. Every bill issued in Great Britain or Northern Ireland to which the Hague Rules apply must contain such a paramount clause.

'... paramount clause is a term of art, and means a clause incorporating the Hague Rules either simpliciter or if, and as, made compulsory by whatever may be the relevant local law.' *Per* Robert Goff LJ in *Nea Agrea SA* v. *Baltic Shipping Co Ltd and Intershipping Charter Co; The Agios Lazaros* [1976] 2 Lloyd's Rep 47 at p. 53.

party and party costs - the costs which a party is entitled to recover by virtue of his being made party to the actions or arbitration reference. Party and party costs include court fees, stamp and the reasonable charges of a solicitor or counsel in the conduct of the case. **See also: costs.**

party-appointed arbitrators - these are arbitrators appointed by the parties in arbitration as opposed to the third arbitrator or umpire who is normally appointed by the party-appointed arbitrators. They are also known as original arbitrators in some institutional administered arbitrations, for example, in LMAA arbitrations. **See: original arbitrators.**

pay arbitrations - a form of industrial arbitrations conducted by virtue of the consent of the parties to settle pay disputes normally subsisting between employers and employees. The award, which is advisory and recommendatory, is not intended by the parties to be legally binding and enforceable. However, parties often agree to be bound by the decisions of the arbitrator before the commencement of these pay arbitrations, frequently upon the insistence of the institutions which organise such references. **See: ACAS, Central Arbitration Committee; industrial arbitration.**

payment into court - a sum paid voluntarily by the defendant into an account in the court to satisfy all or part of the plaintiff's claim, usually without the knowledge of the judge. The plaintiff has the right to accept or reject the payment. If the plaintiff accepts the payment, the action comes to an end and he will also receive his costs. If the plaintiff rejects the payment, and is eventually awarded less than the payment, the defendant usually gets his costs from the plaintiff from the date he makes the payment. In some circumstances, the court may order payment into court. Compare: **offer; sealed offer; 'without prejudice' offer** in arbitration.

PC - Judicial Committee of the Privy Council.

PCA - Permanent Court of Arbitration. **See: Permanent Court of Arbitration.**

Permanent Court of Arbitration (PCA) - a misnomer for a panel of arbitrators established in pursuance of the 1899 Hague Convention to facilitate and promote peaceful arbitration between states. The PCA is neither 'permanent' nor a 'court', for in existence, apart from maintaining a list of arbitrators it only has a bureau at The Hague and a standing administrative council.

In 1962, the Bureau of the PCA elaborated a set of Rules of Arbitration and Conciliation for Settlement of International Disputes between Two Parties of which Only One is a State. However, these Rules have not been widely adopted and the PCA is generally regarded as a failure for since its inception in 1899, it has only heard and decided on eight cases.

Personal Insurance Arbitration Service - an arbitration service provided by the Chartered Institute of Arbitrators in conjunction with the various companies in the insurance sector. The scheme entitles the insured to claim against the insurance company for failure to perform under a contract of insurance through arbitration instead of taking actions in court. This service, however, will only apply to persons resident in the United Kingdom: *Rule 2, Personal Insurance Arbitration Service Rules (1983 Edition), of the Chartered Institute of Arbitrators;* and where claims involved amounts less than £25,000.

The insurance company shall be responsible for all costs of the arbitration except for the claimant's costs of preparing and submitting documents and/or of attending a hearing, which costs shall be at the arbitrator's discretion: *Rule 6, Ibid.*

Generally, the arbitration will be on documents only, unless the arbitrator directs otherwise or upon the request of the claimant for hearing: *Rules 7, 7(v) and 8(iii), Ibid.*

An insurer may only be made a party to an arbitration under this service if a joint application for arbitration by both parties has been made to the Institute on the prescribed application form: *Rule 3, Ibid.*

In the absence of agreement by the parties as to the applicable law, it shall be determined by the arbitrator: *Rule 11, Ibid.*

persuasive authority - an authority derives from a judgment of a court (particularly a court from the Commonwealth countries which have legal systems based upon the common law) or from opinion of publicists contained in textbooks or treatises, which is not binding under the doctrine of precedents (see: *stare decisis;* **precedents**) but nevertheless is appropriate and persuasive to the court in making its judgment. Arbitral award may be persuasive authority but such instances of citing arbitral awards as authorities are rare and unusual.

plaintiff - the person who initiates the actions to seek for relief. Compare: **claimant** in an arbitration reference. **See also: pursuer.**

pleading - written statement served by one party to the other in an action or arbitration. It contains allegations or claims that the party making them proposes to prove at the hearing (but not the evidence by which they are to be proved) and the remedy sought.

The purpose of pleadings is to provide defined issues in the action or reference such that the opposite party has sufficient notice of the other side's case.

pleas-in-law - the Scots term of statement in the Summons or Defences of the legal justification of the claim or defence.

Point of claim- see: **Statement of claim.**

Post Office arbitration - an arrangement between the Chartered Institute of Arbitrators and the Post Office to conduct and administer arbitrations to settle disputes arising out of the loss or damage of inland posts. The scheme, which seeks to provide further dispute settlement facility for the customers of the Post Office, in addition to their statutory rights as consumers, does not apply to overseas post; nor to postal packets to or from the Republic of Ireland, the Channel Islands or the Isle of Man. The arbitration held under this scheme will be governed by the Chartered Institute of Arbitrators Arbitration Arrangements for the Inland Post Rules (1981 Edition), and the arbitrators are appointed by the Institute from amongst its membership.

If legal proceedings under section 30 of the Post Office Act 1969 as amended by the British Telecommunications Act 1981 in respect of alleged loss of or damage to the packet or any of its contents have been commenced by any person, and if the Secretary of the Chartered Institute of Arbitrators is so notified, a request for arbitration under these arrangements will not be accepted, or proceeded with: *Rule 1.5, 1981 Edition.*

A party must claim arbitration within 18 months from the date when the packet was posted.

The arbitration which is on documents only, will be conducted in accordance with English law and the award is legally binding between the parties.

power of arbitrator to correct mistakes - See: **accidental slip or omission;** *functus officio;* **slip rule.**

power of making interlocutory orders - if any party to a reference under an arbitration agreement fails within the time specified in the order or, if no time is so specified, within a reasonable time to comply with an order made by the arbitrator or umpire in the course of the reference, then, on the application of the arbitrator or umpire or of any party to the reference, the High Court may make an order extending such powers of the arbitrator or umpire to make interlocutory orders: *Section 5(1), Arbitration Act 1979.*

The arbitrator or umpire shall have power, to the extent and subject to any conditions specified in the order of the High Court, to continue with the reference in default of appearance or of any other act by one of the parties in like manner as a judge of the High Court might continue with proceedings in that court where a party fails to comply with an order of that court or a requirement of rules of court: *Section 5(2), Arbitration Act 1979.*

practice direction - informal rules of procedure as distinct from those derived from rules of court given occasionally by a judge on the mode of proceeding, e.g., Practice Note in relation to leave to appeal in the Commercial Court given by Bingham J at the sitting of the court: **See:** *[1985] 2 All ER 383.*

precedent - the judgment of the court which becomes binding authority on the lower court. Thus, the decisions of the House of Lords are binding upon the Court of Appeal and all lower courts and are normally followed by the House of Lords itself. The decisions of the Court of Appeal are binding on all the lower courts and, with some exceptions, on itself. Decisions of the High Courts bind the inferior courts, whose decisions do not create binding precedents.

Arbitral awards are usually decided on the authority of judicial precedents although this is not necessarily so. As among the arbitral awards, there has yet to be established a system whereby these awards can be cited as binding precedents in other arbitration references; still less probable is the arbitral awards being cited as precedents in actions in court. **See also: private arbitration.**

preliminary meeting - also known as a 'meeting for directions'. A pre-hearing meeting called by the arbitrator, of all parties to an arbitration so as to formalise and finalise the procedures, arrangements and a time-table for the smooth progress of the arbitration reference. An Order for Directions is usually issued by the arbitrator to both parties after the preliminary meeting. **See also: Order for Directions; liberty to apply.**

preliminary point of law - a question of law submitted to the court for determination before the actual arbitration reference of the disputes has commenced, e.g., question on whether an arbitrator has jurisdiction to sit on the reference.

primary evidence - the best evidence available, e.g., the original of a document. **See also: secondary evidence.**

***prima facie* evidence** - presumptive evidence, i.e., evidence of sufficient weight as to justify a reasonable inference of its existence. It is not however, a conclusive evidence of fact.

principle in *Conquer* v. *Boot* - the principle derived from and named after *Conquer* v. *Boot* [1928] 2 KB 336, which stipulates that damages including anticipated future damages from one and the same cause of action, must be assessed in one proceeding.

principles for removal of arbitrator for misconduct - *Per* Mustill J in *Bremer HmbH* v. *Ets Soules et Cie and Anthony G Scott* [1985] 1 Lloyd's Rep 160 at p. 164: 'there are three material situations in which the High Court has power to remove an arbitrator for "misconduct", under section 23 of the Arbitration Act, 1950.

(1) Where it is proved that the arbitrator suffers from what may be called "actual bias". In this situation, the complaining party satisfies the court that the arbitrator is predisposed to favour one party, or, conversely, to act unfavourably towards him, for reasons peculiar to that party, or to a group of which he is a member. Proof of actual bias entails proof that the arbitrator is in fact incapable of approaching the

issues with the impartiality which his office demands. (See also: actual bias).

(2) Where the relationship between the arbitrator and the parties, or between the arbitrator and the subject-matter of the dispute, is such as to create an evident risk that the arbitrator has been, or will in the future be, incapable of acting impartially. To establish a case of misconduct in this category, proof of actual bias is unnecessary. The misconduct consists of assuming or remaining in office in circumstances where there is a manifest risk of partiality. This may be called a case of "imputed bias". (See also: imputed bias)

(3) Where the conduct of the arbitrator is such as to show that, questions of partiality aside, he is, through lack of talent, experience or diligence, incapable of conducting the reference in a manner which the parties are entitled to expect.'

See: misconduct; legal misconduct; technical misconduct; moral misconduct; removal of arbitrator.

private arbitration - (1) in the past a voluntary submission out of court, which is similar to the present-day consensus arbitration, where parties consented to refer some or all of the issues in a pending suit to arbitration; (2) the common view that arbitration is a private matter. 'The concept of private arbitrations derives simply from the fact that the parties have agreed to submit to arbitration particular disputes arising between them and only between them. It is implicit in this that strangers shall be excluded from the hearing and conduct of the arbitration and that neither the tribunal nor any of the parties can insist that the dispute shall be heard or determined concurrently with or even in consonance with another disputes ...': *Per* Leggatt J in *Oxford Shipping Co Ltd* v. *Nippon Yusen Kaisha, The Eastern Saga* [1984] 2 Lloyd's Rep 373 at p. 379; [1984] 3 All ER 835 at p. 842.

privilege - (1) the right to withhold documentary evidence on the ground of some special interest recognised by the law, e.g., Crown privilege, legal professional privilege; (2) a special right or immunity from suits conferred upon a person by virtue of his office or rank, e.g., the words uttered by Members of Parliament in the House are privileged; An arbitrator acting in a judicial capacity in an arbitration reference is privileged to be immune from suit regarding negligence. **See also: immunity of arbitrator.**

privity - the relationship of the parties by reason of their entering into a contract or participating in some transactions or events. **See: privity of contract.**

privity of contract - the relationship of the parties to a contract in respect of their rights and liabilities. In law of contract, a third party has no cause of action, i.e., to sue and be sued on it against any party of the contract to which he is not a party. However, in relation to arbitration, the court will give effect to an arbitration agreement involving a third party, although there is no privity of contract between the parties: *Northern Regional Health Authority* v. *Derek Crouch Construction Co Ltd* [1984] 2 All ER 175 CA.

procedural law - also known as curial law. The law governing the procedures of the reference. This is often the law of the place where the arbitration is held **(see: *lex loci arbitri*),** unless otherwise specified by the parties: *James Miller & Partners Ltd* v. *Whitworth Street Estates (Manchester) Ltd* [1970] AC 583. The fundamental principle in English rules of private international law is that, in the absence of any contractual provision to the contrary, the procedural law governing arbitration is that of the forum of the arbitration: *Bank Mellat* v. *Helliniki Techniki SA* [1983] 3 All ER 428. In the event that the procedural rule or law is specified, it must be applied in consonance with the local law of the place where the arbitration is held. Therefore, where an arbitration agreement specifies that the procedural law or rule be institutional rules, e.g., ICC Rules, these rules have to be interpreted subject to the local procedural law: *International Tank and Pipe SAK* v. *Kuwait Aviation Fuelling Co KSC* [1975] QB 224.

procedural mishap - (1) the making of an award when it should have been made until a further issue has been heard and determined; (2) the expressing of a view upon that further issue without indicating expressly or by implication that it is a preliminary view: *Hagop*

Ardahalian v. *Unifert International SA; The Elissar* [1984] 1 Lloyd's Rep 206. Contrast: **misconduct.**

procedure - the manner in which court proceedings are conducted. In the absence of express agreement by the parties, an arbitrator need not follow strictly the court procedure in conducting the arbitration. He is the master of the procedure of arbitration, provided that he does not contravene the rules of natural justice. If the parties desire, the arbitrator can conduct the reference under inquisitorial procedure, otherwise he is obliged to conduct the reference under adversary procedure. **See: procedural law; adversary procedure; inquisitorial procedure.**

proof of evidence - a statement listing the evidence which a witness, especially an expert witness, intends to give on oath or affirmation. It usually contains the witness' name and qualification or expertise, the inspection or survey of the subject in dispute, if any, and his opinion and conclusion.

Protection and Indemnity Clubs - mutual clubs exist in the City of London to insure the shipowners' liabilities against the loss of their ships. The clubs are self-regulating markets, in which the shipowners, as members, control their entire affairs without any government or outside intervention.

publication of an award - where notice is given by the arbitrator or umpire to the parties that the award is ready, the award is said to be published.

publication to the parties - publication of an award (as distinct from "publication" of it simply) entails both completion of the award, so that the arbitrator has finally adjudicated and retains no power of altering it, and also notice to the parties that this has been done: *Brooke* v. *Mitchell* (1840) 9 LJ Ex 269. It is immaterial, however, whether or not the parties are then made acquainted with the contents of the award or receive copies of it: *Hemsworth* v. *Brian* (1844) 14 LJ CP 36.

Note: the above quotations are stated in *Russell on Arbitration* at p. 411 (1979 Edn.) and at p. 442 (1982 Edn.) and have been approved by Parker J in *Bulk Transport Corpn* v. *Sissy Steamship Co Ltd; Bulk Transport Corpn* v. *Ifled Shipping Corpn; The Archipelagos and Delfi* [1979] 2 Lloyd's Rep 289 at pp. 293 - 294.

Puisne Judge - a judge of the High Court appointed from amongst barristers of at least ten years' standing. They are normally knighted upon appointment but are referred to as 'Mr Justice ...'

punitive damage - see exemplary damages

pursuer - the Scottish equivalent of claimant or plaintiff.

Q

QBD - Queen's Bench Division. **See: Queen's Bench Division; High Court of Justice.**

QBD (Com Ct) - Queen's Bench Division Commercial Court. **See: Commercial Court.**

QC - Queen's Counsel.

quality arbitration - a form of expert valuation to determine the quality of goods at the port of destination. Hence, it is mostly held in larger sea ports like London, Hamburg, Marseille, Rotterdam, Bremen, etc.

Most quality arbitrations are conducted under the relevant rules of the local trade and import associations.

In quality arbitration, each party commences the proceeding by appointing two experts sometimes known as the 'arbiters'. When the two arbiters fail to agree, an umpire is then appointed either by the two arbiters or by the trade association concerned. However, the decision shall be made by the majority of the three.

The decision of a quality arbitration is not an arbitral award and has no legal force. The party who obtains a favourable decision must seek additional means of enforcing this decision either by arbitration or litigation. Nevertheless, the tribunal called upon to enforce the decision will treat the decision of the quality arbiters as a statement of act, unless this decision has been obtained defectively, e.g., as the result of faulty procedures.

Quality arbitration is a very common form of valuation in the commodity trade. **See also: GAFTA arbitration; FOSFA arbitration.**

quasi - as if it were.

quasi-arbitrator - 'There may be circumstances in which what is in effect an arbitration is not one that is within the provisions of the Arbitration Act. The expression quasi-arbitrator should only be used in that connection. A person will only be an arbitrator or quasi-arbitrator if there is a submission to him either of a specific dispute or of present points of difference or of defined differences that may in future arise and if there is agreement that his decision will be binding': *Per* Lord Morris in *Sutcliffe* v. *Thackrah* [1974] 1 All ER 859 at pp. 876-877.

quasi-judicial function - where function to determine a dispute is exercised by virtue of an executive discretion rather than the application of law.

Queen's Bench Division (QBD) - the division of the High Court which dispenses justice in civil actions based on contract or tort. It also exercises supervisory jurisdiction over all inferior courts and acts as the appellate court. The Commercial Court and the Admiralty Court are part of the Division. When the sovereign is a King, it is known as the King's Bench Division (KBD).

Queen's Bench Master - see: Masters of the Supreme Court.

question of facts - in an arbitration, it is a question for the arbitrator to decide: *Reinante Transoceanic Navegacion SA* v. *The President of India; The Apiliotis* [1985] 1 Lloyd's Rep 255.

Elements of foreign law which arises in English law is usually regarded as a question of fact.

Where an arbitrator makes an error of fact on the face of the award, the High Court shall not have jurisdiction to set aside or remit an award: *Section 1(1), Arbitration Act 1979*. '... there is in many cases (though not in all) the possibility of an appeal from a court on a question of fact, whereas no such appeal lies from an arbitration.' *Per* Robert Goff LJ in *Mutual Shipping Corpn of New York* v. *Bayshore Shipping Co of Monrovia; The Montan* [1985] 1 All ER 520 at p. 529 CA.

question of law - matter which touches on the interpretation and determination of law. For example, the interpretation of a term of a contract, the determination of whether or not an arbitrator has jurisdiction to sit on the reference. Generally, arbitrators have power to decide on question of law. Where an arbitrator makes an error of law on the face of the award, the High Court shall not have jurisdiction to set aside or remit an award: *Section 1(1), Arbitration Act 1979.* However, the parties may appeal to the High Court on any question of law arising out of an award made on an arbitration agreement: *Section 1(2), Arbitration Act 1979.* Such an appeal is only possible if the parties have expressed their consent or the court has granted leave to appeal: *Section 1(3), Arbitration Act 1979.* Where the applicant contends that any question of law arising out of an award concerns a term of contract or an event which is not a one-off clause or event, he shall serve on the respondent with his notice of motion and lodge with the court an affidavit setting out the facts relied on in support of his contention: *Practice Note in relation to leave to appeal in the Commercial Court* [1985] 2 All ER 383. **See also: appeal; leave to appeal;** *Nema* **Guidelines, the; question of facts.**

R

ratio decidendi - principle upon which a case is based. Actual decision in conjunction with the facts material to it.

real evidence - models, maps, plans etc. which are tendered as evidence in a proceeding to illustrate some property or thing involved in the dispute.

reasoned award - an award which, apart from the decision of the arbitrator, contains reasons of how he arrives at his conclusion.
    'No particular form of award is required ... All that is necessary is that the arbitrators should set out what on their view of evidence, did or did not happen, and should explain succinctly why in the light of what happened, they have reached their decision and what that decision is. That is all that is meant by a "reasoned award" ... Where a 1979 [Arbitration] Act award differs from a judgment is in the fact that the arbitrators will not be expected to analyse the law and the authorities. It will be quite sufficient that they should explain how they reached their conclusion. ... [A reasoned award] is not technical, it is not difficult to draw and above all it is something which can and should be produced promptly and quickly at the conclusion of the hearing ...' (*Per* Donaldson LJ in *Bremer Handelsgesellschaft mbH* v. *Westzucker GmbH* [1981] 2 Lloyd's Rep 130 at p. 132.) 'The present position is that an arbitrator can (a) give reasons for his award without any restriction on the use to be made of those reasons, (b) give no reasons or (c) give reasons subject to a restriction.' *(Per* Sir John Donaldson MR in *Mutual Shipping Corpn of New York* v. *Bayshore Shipping Co of Monrovia; The Montan* [1985] 1 All ER 520 CA.) Where reasons for an award are issued at the same time as the award, the court has construed this to mean that the reasons are virtually incorporated into it, even though these reasons are not stapled together with the award: *Pearl Marin Shipping A/B* v. *Pietro Cingolani SAS; The General Valdes* [1982] 1 Lloyd's Rep 17 CA. Where an umpire provides his reasons to an award, in the absence of a disclaimer, the umpire intends to invite the

parties to read his reasons as part of the award: (*ibid.*). However, even if the reasons are marked confidential or restricted, the court can still look at them: *Mutual Shipping Corpn of New York* v. *Bayshore Shipping Co of Monrovia; The Montan* [1985] 1 All ER 520 CA. **See also: claused reasons; confidential reasons.**

recall of witness - the futher examination of a witness who has given his evidence. This practice is permitted by the court to allow evidence in rebuttal.

recitals - that part of the award which sets out the chronology of the events that led to the arbitrator's finding of facts. Recitals are introduced by the word 'WHEREAS'.

Recorder - a barrister or solicitor appointed as part-time judge, sitting at least four weeks a year. Though he usually sits in the Crown Court, he may also sit in the County Court or the High Court.

re-examination - the procedure in the hearing where the witness is examined for the second time by the party which calls him, after he has been cross-examined by the opposite party. The purpose of the re-examination is to elicit facts arising out of the cross-examination. As such, new matter may only be introduced with leave of the judge.

reference - the actual hearing of the matter by the arbitrator in an arbitration.

Registrar of the County Court - a judicial officer appointed by the Lord Chancellor from solicitors of not less than seven years' standing to supervise the interlocutory and post-judgment stage of the case. He can also try cases within a financial limit set by statute.

registration of award - the process of registering a foreign award as a judgment of the High Court for the purpose of enforcing it under section 26 of the Arbitration Act 1950.
    RSC Order 73, r. 8 provides: 'Where an award is made in proceedings on an arbitration in any part of Her Majesty's dominions or

other territory to which Part I of the Foreign Judgments (Reciprocal Enforcement) Act 1933 extends, being a part to which Part II of the Administration of Justice Act 1920 extends immediately before the said Part I was extended thereto, then, if the award has, in pursuance of the law in force in the place where it was made, become enforceable in the same manner as a judgment given by a court in that place. Order 71 shall apply in relation to the award as it applies in relation to a judgment given by that court, subject, however, to the following modifications:-
(a) for references to the country of the original court there shall be substituted references to the place where the award was made; and (b) the affidavit required by rule 3 of the said Order must state (in addition to the other matters required by that rule) that to the best of the information or belief of the deponent the award has, in pursuance of the law in force in the place where it was made, become enforceable in the same manner as a judgment given by a court in that place.'

remedy - redress, relief available at law for the enforcement, protection or recovery of rights or for obtaining redress for their infringement.
Since an arbitration can only be held in respect of certain civil matters, the main remedies given by an arbitral tribunal include specific performance under section 15 of the Arbitration Act 1950 and damages. **See: specific performance; damages.**

remission of award - parties may apply to the High Court or a judge thereof, who has power to remit an award to the reconsideration of the arbitrator or umpire: *Section 22(1), Arbitration Act 1950*. The arbitrator or umpire, unless the court otherwise directs in the order of remission, shall make his award within three months after the date of the order: *Section 22(2), Arbitration Act 1950*. This section 22 places the duty to decide whether or not to remit the matter on the court. It is the court and the court alone which has to decide it: *Aiden Shipping Co Ltd v. Interbulk Ltd; Interbulk Ltd v. ICCO International Corn Co NV; The Vimeira* [1985] 2 Lloyd's Rep 407.
The application for remission of an award must be made by originating motion to the judge of the High Court. Where arbitration to which the Arbitration Act 1979 applies, the application must be made to

the Commercial Judge, unless he otherwise directs: *RSC Order 73, rules 2(1) and (6)*. However, where arbitration is not subject to the 1979 Act, RSC Order 73 r. 6 shall not apply: *Compania Maritima Zorroza SA* v. *Bulk Carriers Corporation* [1980] 2 Lloyd's Rep 186.

'There are four grounds upon which the matter can be remitted to an arbitrator for reconsideration. Those grounds are (1) where the award is bad on the face of it; (2) where there has been misconduct on the part of the arbitrator; (3) where there has been an admitted mistake, and the arbitrator himself asks that the matter may be remitted; and (4) where additional evidence has been discovered after the making of the award.' *Per* Chitty LJ in *re Arbitration between Montomery, Jones & Co and Liebenthal & Co* (1898) 78 LT NS 406 at p. 408.

However, the court nowadays has remitted awards on other wider grounds: See for example, *Compagnie Financière pour le Commerce Exterieur SA* v. *Oy Vahna AB* [1963] 2 Lloyd's Rep 463 CA; *Margulies Bros Ltd* v. *Dafnis Thomaides & Co (UK) Ltd* [1958] 1 All ER 777; *Franz Haniel AG* v. *Sabre Shipping Corpn* [1962] 1 Lloyd's Rep 531; *Universal Cargo Carriers Corpn* v. *Citati* [1957] 3 All ER 234; *European Grain and Shipping Ltd* v. *Cremer* [1983] 1 Lloyd's Rep 211; *Bremer HmbH* v. *Raiffeisen Hauptgenossenschaft EG* [1982] 1 Lloyd's Rep 599 CA; *Hayn Roman & Co SA* v. *Cominter (UK) Ltd* [1982] 2 Lloyd's Rep 458.

Where an award is remitted by the court under paragraph b of section 1(2) of the Arbitration Act 1979, the arbitrator or umpire shall, unless the order of the court otherwise directs, make his award within three months after the date of the order: *Section 1(2)(b), Arbitration Act 1979*.

The effect of an order to remit an award for reconsideration by the arbitrator or umpire is akin to a retrial in an action in court.

removal of arbitrator - the revocation by the court of the arbitrator's appointment to conduct the reference on the grounds that the arbitrator has misconducted himself or the proceeding: *Section 23(1), Arbitration Act 1950*.

An arbitrator will be removed if he acts unfairly and without impartiality between the parties: *re An Arbitration between the owners of Steamship Catalina & others and the owners of motor vessel Norma* (1938) 61 Ll LR 360.

An arbitrator will be removed if he fails to conduct the arbitration in accordance with the principles of natural justice: *A Fox* v. *P G Wellfair Ltd; Fisher* v. *P G Wellfair Ltd* [1981] 2 Lloyd's Rep 514 CA.

Where an arbitrator allows the arbitration to be reduced to such a state that there is no prospect of justice being done if it continues and there is a virtual certainty that injustice will be done to one party, the arbitrator will be removed: *Pratt* v. *Swanmore Builders Ltd & Baker* [1980] 2 Lloyd's Rep 504.

Whether an arbitrator should be removed on ground of imputed bias depends on three tests: that the test is objective; that the reasonable man forms his view with no inside knowledge; and that there is a real likelihood of bias: *Tracomin SA* v. *Gibbs Nathaniel (Canada) Ltd & George Jacob Bridge* [1985] 1 Lloyd's Rep 586.

Where all the arbitrators of a tribunal are being removed, the court shall, on the application of any party, appoint a person or persons to act as arbitrator or arbitrators in place of the person or persons so removed: *Section 25(1), Arbitration Act 1950.* However, if all the arbitrators in a tribunal are removed, then the court may appoint a person to act as sole arbitrator in place of the person or persons removed: *Section 25(2)(a), Arbitration Act 1950,* or order that the arbitration agreement shall cease to have effect with respect to the dispute referred: *Section 25(3)(b), Arbitration Act 1950.*

See also: principles for removal of arbitrator for misconduct.

rent review clause - a provision in a lease specifying in what manner and by whom the rent shall be determined when the parties are unable to agree between themselves. It usually provides for a reference to an arbitrator at the election of the tenant by a counter-notice served not later than a certain period of months after the landlord's trigger notice, time being expressly made of the essence. Such a clause is very popular as a standard provision in a lease nowadays. It has been held in *United Scientific Holdings Ltd* v. *Barnley Borough Council* [1978] AC 904 that the rent review clause confers privilege to both the landlord and the tenant. Thus the clause has generally been regarded as an arbitration clause. However, in a recent case of *Tote Bookmakers Ltd* v. *Development and Property Holding Co Ltd* [1985] 2 All ER 555 it is held by the court that the rent review clause cannot amount to an arbitration agreement because it does not give bilateral right of reference to the parties. **See also: arbitration agreement.**

repudiation - the principle of anticipatory breach under the law of contract. In relation to arbitration agreement, repudiation may include one of the following sets of circumstances: (i) conduct of a party showing his intention not to arbitrate; or (ii) inability of a party to perform his obligation to arbitrate: *Universal Cargo Carriers Corpn* v. *Pedro Citati* [1958] 2 Lloyd's Rep 17; or (iii) verbal renunciation of the arbitration agreement; or (iv) a breach of the arbitration agreement as to go to the root of the contract. **See also: anticipatory breach.**

res judicata pro veritate accipitur - a thing adjudicated is received as the truth. In relation to arbitration, once a domestic award is made, it is *res judicata* in respect of the matter decided. Thus, in an action on enforcing the award, it is the party denying the validity of the award who should prove. **See also: enforcement of arbitral award.**

respondent- the party who defends or responds to the claim in an arbitration reference. Compare: defendant in an action in court.

restricted reasons - see: **claused reasons; confidential reasons.**

reversal of judgment - where judgment or decision of the lower court is being altered, either wholly or partly, on appeal. Compare: **remission of award; setting aside of award** in arbitration.

revocation of appointment of arbitrator - unless a contrary intention is expressed in the agreement the authority of an arbitrator is not revocable except by leave of the High Court or a judge thereof: *Section 1, Arbitration Act 1950*. However, where an arbitrator is put to question in respect of his misconduct or of the proceedings or of fraud, such that he is not, or may not be impartial, the court may revoke his authority as the arbitrator: *Sections 13(3), 23(1) and 24(2) Arbitration Act 1950.*

RSC - Rules of the Supreme Court. **See: Rules of the Supreme Court.**

RSC Order 73, rule 6 - introduced to operate from 1979. *Applications and Appeals to be heard by Commercial Judges* (1) any matter which is required, by rules 2 and 3, to be heard by a judge, shall be heard by a Commercial Judge, unless any such judge otherwise directs; (2) nothing in the foregoing paragraph shall be construed as preventing the powers of a Commercial Judge from being exercised by any judge of the High Court. **See also: commercial judges.**

In the case of arbitrations which are not governed by Arbitration Act 1979 (i.e., those arbitrations which commenced before 1 August 1979 the date on which the Arbitration Act 1979 came into operation and that the parties have not agreed in writing that the Arbitration Act 1979 should apply), RSC Order 72, r. 6 is as follows: '6. *Transfer of certain applications, etc. to the Commercial list* (1) an application in proceedings in the Queen's Bench Division to transfer to the Commercial list - (a) a special case stated for the decision of the High Court by an arbitrator or umpire under section 21 of the Arbitration Act 1950; or (b) any such application is referred to in rule 5(1); may be made to the judge in charge of the Commercial list by summons, and if it appears to the judge that the subject-matter of the reference or award to which such case or application relates is of a commercial nature, he may make an order transferring the case or application to the Commercial list; (2) Order 72, rules 2(3) and (4) and 6(1) shall apply in relation to a special case or application transferred to the Commercial list by order under this rule as they apply to actions in the Commercial list.

rules of court - those rules formulated by a rule committee to regulate the practice and procedure in court. **See: Rules of the Supreme Court.**

Rules of the Supreme Court (RSC) - the rules formulated by the Supreme Court Rule Committee, which govern and regulate the practice and procedure in the Supreme Court of Judicature. The Rules have 114 Orders catering for all aspects of procedures relating to the High Court and the Court of Appeal.

Order 73 of the RSC is especially formulated to apply to arbitration proceedings in relation to matter or cause consisting of an application to the High Court or a judge thereof under the Arbitration Acts 1950-1979.

S

Salvage arbitration - see: **Lloyd's Form Arbitration.**

Scott Schedule - otherwise known as an 'Official Referee's Schedule', is a schedule to summarise a claim which comprises a large number of items each of which has a separate basis in the contract. It does not have a fixed format except that the claims are itemised with the contentions of both parties listed.

Scott v. *Avery* **Clause** - a type of arbitration clause named after *Alexander Scott* v. *George Avery* (1856) 10 ER 1121, which establishes that parties can make arbitration reference a condition precedent to the right of action in court. (See: **condition precedent**). An example of the clause: 'It shall be a condition precedent to any right of action or suit upon this policy that the award by such arbitrator, arbitrators or umpire of the amount of loss or damage if disputes shall be first obtained.' See also: **GAFTA arbitration clause.**

A *Scott* v. *Avery* clause postpones but does not annihilate the right of the parties of access to actions in court: *General Electricity Board* v. *Halifax Corpn* [1963] AC 785. The court must give effect to a *Scott* v. *Avery* clause unless there is a waiver: *Heyman and another* v. *Darwins Ltd* [1942] AC 356. *Scott* v. *Avery* clause, although it is one-sided in its operation and confers advantages or liberties onto one party only, nevertheless, is in essence mere machinery to settle disputes, even if it be one-sided machinery: *Woolfe* v. *Collis Removal Service* [1947] 2 All ER 260. The clause may even bind a third party: *Freshwater* v. *Western Australian Assurance Co Ltd* [1933] 1 KB 515.

See also: **arbitration agreement.**

sealed offer - an offer to settle which is contained in a letter and sealed in an envelope and handed to the arbitrator during the reference.

'A "sealed offer" is the arbitral equivalent of making a payment into court in settlement of the litigation or of particular causes of action in that litigation. Neither the fact, nor the amount, of such a payment into court can be revealed to the judge trying the case until he has given judgment on all matters other than costs. As it is customary for an award to deal at one and the same time both with the parties' claims and with the question of costs, the existence of a sealed offer has to be brought to the attention of the arbitrator before he has reached a decision. However it should remain sealed at that stage and it would be wholly improper for the arbitrator to look at it before he has reached a final decision on the matters in dispute other than as to costs, or to revise that decision in the light of the terms of the sealed offer when he sees them.' *Per* Donaldson J in *Tramountana Armadora SA* v. *Atlantic Shipping Co SA* [1978] 2 All ER 870 at p. 876. The question of costs in relation to the sealed offer is entirely within the discretion of the arbitrators: *Argolis Shipping Co SA* v. *Midwest Steel and Alloy Corpn; The Angeliki* [1982] 2 Lloyd's Rep 594.

See also: **open offer; 'without prejudice' offer.**

secondary evidence - evidence such as a copy of the original document, that by its nature suggests that better evidence is available. It can be rejected if it is proved that primary evidence is available. Otherwise, it is generally admissible if the absence of the primary evidence has been supported by satisfactory explanation. **See also: primary evidence.**

second-hand evidence - see: **hearsay evidence.**

section 27, Arbitration Act 1950 - See: **extension of time.**

security for costs - the guarantee provided by the claimant in an arbitration reference to meet the costs if he fails in his claim. An order for security for costs may only be granted to a respondent if he has reason to believe that the claimant will not be in a position to meet the costs or is ordinarily resident abroad: *RSC Order 23, r. 1(1)(a),* or if the claimant is a limited company, it will not be able to pay the costs of the respondents: *Companies Act 1948, section 447.*

Unless otherwise agreed by the parties, the arbitrator has no power to order security for costs: *Re Unione Stearinerie Lanza and*

Wiener [1917] 2 KB 558; *Mavani* v. *Ralli Bros Ltd* [1973] 1 WLR 468. The court has power to order security for costs under section 12(6)(a) of the Arbitration Act 1950. But this power is discretionary: *Sir Lindsay Parkinson & Co Ltd* v. *Triplan Ltd* [1973] 2 All ER 273 CA. 'The English courts should be slow in applying the jurisdiction to order security for costs in international arbitration unless, in the particular circumstances of each case, there is some more specific connection with this country ... than the mere fact that the parties have agreed that any arbitration is to take place in England ...' *Per* Kerr LJ in *Bank Mellat* v. *Helliniki Techniki SA* [1983] 3 All ER 428 CA.

The rule of practice for the court to exercise its discretion to grant an order for security for costs is the same in both an arbitration and an action: *Hudson Strumpffabrik GmbH* v. *Bentley Engineering Co Ltd* [1962] 2 QB 587.

service - the delivery of a writ, summons or other document in a court proceeding, or an arbitration reference.

In general, the method of service of documents in an arbitration is to be in accordance with the provision, if any, of the arbitration agreement. However, in the absence of express stipulation, the manner of service of documents follows the practice of the court proceedings.

In relation to the service of the notice to appoint an arbitrator. Section 34(4) of the Limitation Act 1980 provides that: 'any such notice may be served either - (a) by delivering it to the person on whom it is to be served; or (b) by leaving it at the usual or last-known place of abode in England and Wales of that person; or (c) by sending it by post in a registered letter addressed to that person at his usual or last-known place of abode in England and Wales, as well as in any other manner provided in the arbitration agreement.

The service of notice to commence an arbitration can be given by other methods such as by telex: *NV Stoomv Meats "De Maas"* v. *Nippon Yusen Kaisha; The Pendrecht* [1980] 2 Lloyd's Rep 56 at p. 64.

service out of the jurisdiction - the service of the originating process, such as originating summons, outside the jurisdiction of England and Wales. This service is only permissible with the leave of the court if the applicant can show that the jurisdiction of the English courts has some particular connection with either the defendant or the subject-matter of the proceedings.

In relation to arbitration, RSC Order 73, r. 7 provides:-

'(1) Service out of the jurisdiction - (a) of an originating summons for the appointment of an arbitrator or umpire or for leave to enforce an award; or (b) of notice of an originating motion to remove an arbitrator or umpire or to remit or set aside an award; or (c) of an originating summons or notice of an originating motion under the Arbitration Act 1979; or (d) of any order made on such a summons or motion as aforesaid,

is permissible with the leave of the court provided that the arbitration to which the summons, motion or order relates is governed by English law or has been, is being, or is to be held, within the jurisdiction.

(2) An application for the grant of leave under this rule must be supported by an affidavit stating the grounds on which the application is made and showing in what place or country the person to be served is, or probably may be found; and no such leave shall be granted unless it shall be made sufficiently to appear to the court that the case is a proper one for service out of the jurisdiction under this rule.

(3) Order 11, rules 5, 6 and 8, shall apply in relation to any such summons, notice or order as is referred to in paragraph (1) as they apply in relation to notice of a writ.'

setting aside of award - where an arbitrator or umpire has misconducted himself or the proceedings, or an arbitration, or award has been improperly procured, the High Court may set aside the award: *Section 23(2), Arbitration Act 1950.*

The application for setting aside an award must be made by notice of originating motion to the judge of the High Court. Where arbitration to which the Arbitration Act 1979 applies, the application must be made to the Commercial Judge, unless he otherwise directs and the notice of originating motion must be served within 21 days after the award has been made and published to the parties: *RSC Order 73, r. 5(1) and r. 6.* **See also: publication of an award.**

Once an award is set aside, it shall cease to have legal effect i.e., it shall not be enforceable under section 26 of the Arbitration Act 1950.

In the absence of judicial authority, it is not certain in the event of an order to set aside the award whether the arbitral tribunal is being rendered *functus officio* by the court. If the arbitrator is removed (under section 23(1) of the Arbitration Act 1950) and the award is set aside, any subsequent arbitration would be akin to a new trial in the actions in court, as opposed to a re-trial by the same tribunal as in the case of remission. If the arbitrator is not removed but only the award is set aside it is submitted that the effect of the setting aside of the award is theoretically the same as in the case of remission of award. **See also: remission of award.**

Shelltime 3 Form arbitration clause - one of the most common forms of arbitration clause used in shipping industry. '(a) this charter shall be construed and the relations between the parties determined in accordance with the law of England; (b) any dispute arising under this charter shall be decided by the English courts to whose jurisdiction the parties agree whatever their domicile may be: Provided that either party may elect to have the dispute referred to the arbitration of a single arbitrator in London in accordance with the provisions of the Arbitration Act 1950, or any statutory modification or re-enactment thereof for the time being in force. Such election shall be made by written notice by one party to the other not later than 21 days after receipt of a notice given by one party to the other of a dispute having arisen under this charter.'

shipping arbitration - see: **maritime arbitration.**

sine die - without a day. Indefinite adjournment.

single arbitrator tribunal - see: **sole-arbitrator tribunal.**

slip rule - a rule that clerical mistake, accidental omissions etc., in judgment and orders may be corrected by the court at any time on application by motion or summons: *RSC Order 20, r. 11.* The power under the slip rule cannot be exercised to enable a tribunal 'to reconsider a final and regular decision once it has been perfected.' *Per* Sir John Donaldson MR in *R* v. *Cripps, ex p Muldoon* [1984] 2 All ER 705 at

p. 710; [1984] 1 QB 686 at p. 695. In relation to arbitral awards, such mistakes and omissions may be corrected under section 17 of the Arbitration Act 1950. 'I have no doubt that an arbitrator has the same power to correct errors under section 17 as the High Court has to correct errors under Order 20, r. 11. The difference between the powers of an arbitrator and the powers of the High Court is that the former lacks the inherent jurisdiction of the court to rectify an order, so as to make it accord with the intention of the court. As, however, an arbitrator draws up his own award, the only mistake in the actual drawing up of the award is likely to be a clerical error which he can himself correct under section 17. It is true that, when a judge of the High Court makes an obvious error, counsel may observe it and draw the matter to the attention of the court for correction before the order is drawn up, whereas, since an arbitrator becomes *functus officio* at the moment when he publishes his award, that opportunity is not available in arbitrations;' *Per* Robert Goff LJ in *Mutual Shipping Corpn of New York* v. *Bayshore Shipping Co of Monrovia; The Montan* [1985] 1 All ER 520 at p. 529 CA.

sole arbitrator - the one and only arbitrator sitting in the arbitration reference. **See: sole-arbitrator tribunal.**

sole-arbitrator tribunal - an arbitration reference conducted by one arbitrator, under the following circumstances: (1) as provided by the arbitration agreement; (2) where the agreement provides for two arbitrators to hear the reference, one arbitrator is appointed but not the second one. Thus, the arbitrator appointed is being instructed to proceed as sole arbitrator; (3) where the agreement does not provide for a sole arbitrator or otherwise, then reference is to a sole arbitrator: *Section 6 of the Arbitration Act 1950.*

Where a sole arbitrator is to be appointed by the parties and they fail to agree on any; where the appointed sole arbitrator dies, refuses to act, or becomes incapable of acting and the parties cannot agree on his successor; or where the appointing body fails or refuses to appoint an arbitrator within seven days of receiving written notice to appoint from one of the parties, the court will appoint one on application: *Section 10, Arbitration Act 1950.*

Solicitors Arbitration Scheme - an arbitration scheme, which is administered by the Chartered Institute of Arbitrators and set up at the request of The Law Society. This scheme operates to resolve disputes over negligence between solicitors in England and Wales and their clients, involving claims however small. In this respect, it excludes the settlement of differences touching on fees, accounts and allegation of solicitor's dishonesty or other professional misconduct. Prior consent must be obtained from the solicitor concerned before an arbitration can be held under this scheme. Where parties agree to refer disputes to arbitration under this scheme, the arbitration will be governed by the Rules on Solicitors Arbitration Scheme of the Chartered Institute of Arbitrators (1986 Edition) and subject to the Arbitration Acts 1950-1979.

Subject to any direction issued by the arbitrator, who is appointed by the Chartered Institute of Arbitrators, the arbitration will be on documents only: *Rules 7 and 8(vii), Rules on Solicitors Arbitration Scheme of the Chartered Institute of Arbitrators (1986 Edition).*

The award rendered by the arbitrator is final and binding on the parties, subject to the right of appeal to the court as warranted under the Arbitration Acts 1950-1979: *Rules 15 and 16, (Ibid.).*

If the arbitrator awards against the solicitor, the claimant shall enforce the award by first claiming from the solicitor concerned. But if the solicitor fails to act, the claimant shall inform the Secretary, Professional Purposes, The Law Society, 113 Chancery Lane, London WC2A 1PL, who will take up the matter with the solicitor.

This scheme first came into operation in 1986.

special case procedure - see: case stated. By showing that there is a real and substantial point of law appropriate for decision by a court such that the resolution of which is necessary for the proper determination of the case, the court may make order to direct the arbitrator to state such a case: *Halfdan Grieg & Co A/S* v. *Sterling Coal & Navigation Corpn* [1973] QB 843. With the repeal of section 21 of the Arbitration Act 1950 by section 10 of the Arbitration Act 1979, this special case procedure is rapidly becoming obsolete.

special damages - see damages.

Special Referees - arbitrators specially chosen to sit on the Order 36 references, by virtue of their expertise connected with the subject-matter of the dispute. They possess equal power with the Official Referees during the reference. The parties cannot choose a particular Special Referee but they can challenge the Special Referee's appointment as an arbitrator on any valid ground. **See also: Order 36 Reference; Official Referees.**

special submission - an agreement to refer specific disputes or matters in dispute to arbitration. In this respect, the arbitrator's jurisdiction is narrower than that in the case of general submission.

specialised arbitration - an arbitration touching on specialised matters or subjects which requires persons with specialised knowledge to be appointed as arbitrators, e.g., commodity or maritime arbitrations.

specific performance - a discretionary order given by the court to direct a person to perform his obligation under a contract.

Under section 15 of the Arbitration Act 1950, an arbitrator has the same power as the High Court to order specific performance, unless there is a contrary intention expressed in the arbitration agreement.

stare decisis - a Latin maxim meaning to stand by things decided, i.e., the same point appeared in an action should be treated in the same way as it has been decided earlier in another case. *Stare decisis* forms the basis of the doctrine of precedent, which establishes common law.

In arbitration reference, unless otherwise provided by the parties, the arbitrator need not follow the principle of *stare decisis*. In other words, other arbitral awards, even if cited, are not authorities in relation to the disputes in question, though they may have persuasive force. This is distinct from the application of *stare decisis* in an action in court. **See also: precedent, persuasive authority.**

state further reasons for arbitrator's award, to - the provisions of the Arbitration Act 1979 contain no requirement to mandate an award to be accompanied by reasons or to contain reasons. However, in the event of appeal against the award, the court may order the arbitrator or umpire to state the reasons for his award in sufficient detail so as to enable the court to consider any question of law arising out of the award: *Section 1(5), Arbitration Act 1979.* See for example: *Vermala Shipping Enterprises Ltd* v. *The Minerals and Metals Trading Corpn of India* [1982] 1 Lloyd's Rep 469; *Italmare Shipping Co* v. *Tropwood AG* [1982] 2 Lloyd's Rep 441; *Stinnes Interoil* v. *A Halcoussis & Co* [1982] 2 Lloyd's Rep 445; *Hayn Roman & Co SA* v. *Cominter (UK) Ltd* [1982] 2 Lloyd's Rep 458.

In any case where an award is made without any reason being given, the High Court shall not make an order under section 1(5) of the Arbitration Act 1979 unless it is satisfied: (a) that before the award was made one of the parties to the reference gave notice to the arbitrator or umpire concerned that a reasoned award would be required; or (b) that there is some special reason why such a notice was not given: *Section 1(6), Arbitration Act 1979.* **See also: reasoned award.**

Statement of Claim - a written pleading served by the plaintiff in an action in the High Court. It consists of Points of Claim, Points of Defence and Points of Reply. In arbitration reference, the service of the statement of claim usually follows the manner as if it is an action in court, unless otherwise agreed by the parties in the arbitration agreement or during the preliminary meeting. **See also: preliminary meeting.**

statutory arbitration - arbitration held under the provisions of some Acts of Parliament. 'The arbitral tribunal and its jurisdictions is defined not by any choice or agreement of the parties but by the statute itself. The element of choice is simply the choice of the claimant who chooses to make a claim before the arbitral tribunal. Such a situation is, therefore, more accurately described as one where the claimant invokes the jurisdiction of the tribunal and the respondent submits to it.' *Per* Hobhouse J in *Dallal* v. *Bank Mellat* [1986] 1 All ER 239 at p. 251.

For example, under the Lands Tribunal Act 1949, cases of disputed compensation for compulsory purchase and certain matters under the Land Compensation Acts 1961 and 1973 are referred to the Lands Tribunal which consists of a President and such other members appointed by the Lord Chancellor. Whereas the general conduct of the hearing is at the discretion of the tribunal, the arbitration procedures are usually followed. Thus, the general rule is that Arbitration Acts 1950-1979 will apply to the proceedings save in the case where the applications of the 1950-1979 Acts have been specifically excluded (e.g., under the Agricultural Holdings Act) or that the provisions of the Arbitration Acts 1950-1979 are inconsistent with the particular statute (e.g., in the manner of appointment of the arbitrators): *Section 31(1), Arbitration Act 1950*. Furthermore, section 31(2) of the Arbitration Act 1950 provides that certain sections of it shall not apply to statutory arbitrations. They are as follows:-

Section 2(1): arbitration agreement not to be discharged by death of any party. Section 3: provisions in relation to bankruptcy. Section 5: reference of interpleader issues to arbitration. Section 18(3): provisions in an arbitration agreement regarding costs. Section 24: power of court to give relief where arbitrator is not impartial or the dispute involves question of fraud. Section 25: Power of court where arbitrator is removed or authority of arbitrator is revoked. Section 27: power of court to extend time for commencing arbitration proceedings. Section 29: extension of section 497 of Merchant Shipping Act 1894.

stay of proceedings - where there is a submission to arbitration, any party to the arbitration agreement commences any legal proceedings, the other party may apply to the court for a stay of proceedings in court: *Section 4(1), Arbitration Act 1950*. However, this section does not apply to an arbitration agreement which is not one of domestic arbitration agreement: *Section 1(2), Arbitration Act 1975*. **See also: domestic arbitration agreement;** *lis alibi pendens*.

steps in the proceedings - something in the nature of an application to the court and not mere talk between solicitors or solicitor's clerks, nor the writing of letters, but the taking of some steps, such as taking out a summons or something of that kind, which is, in the technical sense, a step in the proceedings: *Ives & Barker* v. *Williams* [1894] 2 Ch 478. By filling the affidavit to show cause why judgment should not be entered and by appearing before the master amount to taking steps in the proceedings: *Turner & Goudy (a firm)* v. *McConnell and another* [1985] 2 All ER 34.

string arbitration - a form of cost-saving arbitration peculiar to the GAFTA Rules and several other commodity associations. Where there are a string of buyers and sellers of the same commodity, each buying and selling on identical terms except the price, disputes arising and connected therewith may be settled through arbitration between the first seller and the last buyer. All the other parties are named in the same one award as 'intervening principals'. For an example, see: *Burkett Sharpe & Co* v. *Eastcheap Dried Fruit Co and Perera* [1961] 2 Lloyd's Rep 80.
 See also: GAFTA arbitration.

submission - a term used to describe arbitration agreement or an agreement to refer the disputes to arbitration. It is a general agreement (as opposed to special submission) to submit to arbitration the settlement of *all disputes*. Prior to the Arbitration Act 1950, 'submission' was a common term for arbitration agreement. The term is now occasionally used. **See also: special submission; arbitration agreement.**

subpoena - a court order on a person to appear in court to give evidence. He who fails to comply with a subpoena is guilty of contempt of court.
 There are two kinds of subpoena: *subpoena ad testificandum* (requiring him to give evidence) and *subpoena duces tecum* (requiring him to produce certain documents as evidence).
 In relation to arbitration, an arbitrator has no power to order subpoena unless otherwise authorised by the parties. But any party who wishes to compel the attendance of a person to give evidence or requiring him to produce documents as evidence may sue out a writ of *subpoena ad testificandum* or a writ of *subpoena duces tecum* from the High Court: *Section 12(4), Arbitration Act 1950*. Thus failure to comply with such an order amounts to contempt of court rather than of the arbitral tribunal.

subpoena ad testificandum - (Latin) requiring him to give evidence. **See: subpoena.**

subpoena duces tecum - (Latin) requiring him to produce certain documents as evidence. **See: subpoena.**

substantive law - the governing law of the merits of the disputes or the actual law as opposed to adjectival or procedural law. The parties in an arbitration reference are free to choose whichever law as the substantive law.

'An agreement to refer disputes to arbitration in a particular country may carry with it, and is capable of carrying with it, an implication or inference that the parties have further agreed that the law governing the contract ... is to be the law of that country. But I cannot agree that this is a necessary or irresistible inference or implication; there is no inflexible or conclusive rule to the effect that an agreement to refer disputes to arbitration in a particular country carries with it the additional agreement or necessarily indicates a clear intention that the law governing the matters in disputes is to be the law of that country.' *Per* Lord Morris of Borth-y-Gest in *Compagnie d'Armement Maritime SA v. Compagnie Tunisienne de Navigation SA* [1971] AC 572 HL at p. 588.

Where the parties make no reference to the choice of substantive law, all indications must be considered in deciding as to the intention of the parties. (*Ibid.*).

sue - to make a civil claim for a remedy in the court by issuing court proceedings. **See also: claim.**

suit - a general term denoting court proceeding. To bring suit means to pursue the appropriate remedy by the appropriate procedure. In English law, the word 'suit' in Article III r. 6 of the Hague Rules includes arbitrations: see the speech of Davies LJ in *The Merak* [1964] 2 Lloyd's Rep 527 at p. 535.

superior courts - the House of Lords, the Court of Appeal, the High Court and the Crown Court, the Judicial Committee of the Privy Council and certain courts of special jurisdiction, e.g., Restrictive Practices Courts. The decisions of the superior courts carry the weight as judicial precedents.

T

taxation of costs - the examination and investigation of bills of costs to produce true costs by reducing excessive charges and disallowing improper expenses. In arbitration reference, the taxation of costs is either done by the arbitrator *(section 18(1), Arbitration Act 1950)* or by a taxing master of the High Court *(section 18(2), Arbitration Act 1950)*. The arbitrator's own fees are liable to taxation and subject to review in the same manner as taxation of costs *(section 19(3), Arbitration Act 1950)*.

taxing master - an official of the Supreme Court of Judicature in charge of taxation of costs. He is normally a solicitor appointed by the Lord Chancellor. **See also: taxation of costs.**

technical arbitration - a form of dispute settlement based on the evaluation of subject of dispute i.e., the so-called 'smell and feel' arbitration, rather than the evidence and opinion of the parties. It is closer to arbitration *in rem* than *in personam* and akin to certification.

The arbitrator reaches his conclusion by judging at the sample of product submitted to him in the manner prescribed by the relevant rules and code of practice. **See also: quality arbitration.**

technical misconduct - the arbitrator's failure or refusal to perform when requested by the parties. Compare: **misconduct; moral misconduct.**

Failure to award any interest or to deal with interest when there is a claim, and where there is sufficient information before the tribunal to award interest constitutes technical misconduct of the arbitrator: *P J Van Der Zijden Wildhandel NV* v. *Tucker & Cross Ltd* [1976] 1 Lloyd's Rep 341.

Refusal to state their award in the form requested by the parties is technical misconduct of the arbitrators: *The Food Corpn of India* v. *Carras (Hellas) Ltd ; The Dione* [1980] 2 Lloyd's Rep 577. Where an issue is an unpleaded one, an arbitrator commits technical misconduct if he decides on it: *Interbulk Ltd* v. *Aiden Shipping Co Ltd; ICCO International Corn Co NV* v. *Interbulk Ltd; The Vimeira* [1984] 2 Lloyd's Rep 66. Arbitrator's signing of an award without participating in the reference is technical misconduct: *European Grain & Shipping Ltd* v. *Johnston* [1982] 3 All ER 989. It is not technical misconduct if an arbitrator adopts his own process of reasoning to reach a conclusion: *Mabanaft GmbH* v. *Consentine Shipping Co SA; The Achillet* [1984] 2 Lloyd's Rep 191.

terms of reference - arbitration agreement in general. Where parties agreed to submit certain possible or future disputes to arbitration, the terms of reference may be very short and simple, normally expressing clearly the parties' intention to resort to arbitration under certain rules, if provided, for settlement of their disputes. Where parties agreed to submit certain present disputes to arbitration, the terms of reference may be more detailed. In the latter case, the terms of reference form the jurisdiction of the arbitrator. Any decision outside the scope of the terms will be *ultra vires* and null and void, unless otherwise authorised under the Arbitration Acts 1950-1979, if applicable.

trade arbitrator - an arbitrator who is appointed ot sit in a trade arbitration reference. He is normally required to be in the trade to which the dispute relates as a 'commercial man'. **See also: GAFTA arbitration; FOSFA arbitration; commercial man.**

trade dispute - an industrial dispute between an employer and an employee, regarding the employee's employment such as the terms and conditions of employment, pay award, etc. The dispute is normally resolved by ACAS or other industrial tribunals or if the parties so agree, by legal arbitration or by any action in court. **See also: ACAS; Central Arbitration Committee; industrial arbitration.**

U

ultra vires - beyond the power possessed. An act which is outside the powers of authority conferred by law is therefore invalid. **See also: terms of reference.**

umpire - another term used to describe an arbitrator. In a two-member arbitral tribunal, he is appointed by the two arbitrators to settle the dispute between the parties in lieu of the two arbitrators when the arbitrators are unable to agree upon an award. Although most arbitration agreements or clauses provide that the arbitral tribunal shall consist of three members viz., two arbitrators each appointed by one party and the third arbitrator or umpire to be appointed by the two arbitrators, the appointment of an umpire is not a condition precedent to the reference: *Royal Commission on Sugar Supply* v. *Trading Society Kwik Hoo Tong* (1922) 11 Ll LR 163; and that the umpire need not be appointed unless and until the two arbitrators disagree: *Termarea SRL* v. *R Sally* [1979] 2 All ER 989.

The authority of an umpire appointed by or by virtue of an arbitration agreement shall, unless a contrary intention is expressed in the agreement, be irrevocable except by leave of the High Court or a judge thereof: *Section 1 of the Arbitration Act 1950.*

In virtue of section 9 of the Arbitration Act 1979, the sole decision of the umpire is no longer representative of the award of a three-member tribunal; the award of any two of the arbitrators shall be binding.

See also: Judge-umpire.

UNCITRAL - United Nations Commission on International Trade Law. **See: UNCITRAL Model Law on International Commercial Arbitration.**

UNCITRAL arbitration clause - 'any dispute, controversy or claim arising out of or relating to this contract, or the breach, termination or invalidity thereof, shall be settled by arbitration in accordance with the UNCITRAL Arbitration Rules as at present in force.

Note - Parties may wish to consider adding : (a) the appointing authority shall be ... (name of institution or person); (b) the number of arbitrators shall be ... (one or three); (c) the place of arbitration shall be ... (town or country); (d) the language(s) to be used in the arbitral proceedings shall be ...'

UNCITRAL Conciliation Rules - the General Assembly of the United Nations adopted the United Nations Commission on International Trade Law (UNCITRAL) Conciliation Rules on 4 December 1980 to facilitate the settlement of commercial disputes through conciliation. (See UN Resolution 35/52 of 4 December 1980). The provisions are: Article 1 - application of the rules. Article 2 - commencement of conciliation proceedings. Article 3 - number of conciliators. Article 4 - appointment of conciliators. Article 5 - submission of statement to conciliator. Article 6 - representation and assistance. Article 7 - power of conciliator. Article 8 - administrative assistance. Article 9 - communication between conciliators and parties. Article 10 - disclosure of information. Article 11 - co-operation of parties with conciliators. Article 12 - suggestions by parties for settlement of dispute. Article 13 - settlement agreement. Article 14 - confidentiality. Article 15 - termination of conciliation proceedings. Article 16 - resort to arbitral or court proceedings. Article 17 - costs. Article 18 - deposits. Article 19 - role of conciliator in other proceedings. Article 20 - admissibility of evidence in other proceedings.

UNCITRAL Model Law on International Commercial Arbitration - the recent attempt of the UNCITRAL to develop and streamline a uniform system of law in respect of international commercial arbitration. The idea was first mooted in June 1981 at the 14th Session of the UNCITRAL held in Vienna, where Document A/CN 9/207 entitled: 'Possible features of a model law on international commercial arbitration' was presented.

undue hardship - 'Hardship is caused when a justifiable claim which may succeed is barred by a time limit. Undue hardship is caused when the hardship is not warranted by circumstances. I cannot see that the cashflow of a trading applicant, which can never be a safe guide to the means of the applicant or otherwise to his prosperity, is a decisive matter in relation to the consideration of the exercise of discretion. Otherwise, every large company or wealthy individual would be unable to invoke section 27 (of the Arbitration Act 1950) however monstrous the circumstances.' *Per* Peter Gibson J in *Tote Bookmakers v. Development Holding* [1985] 2 All ER 555 at p. 561. '"Undue" does not merely mean "excessive", it means "undeserved" and "unmerited" *Per* Geoffrey Lane LJ in *Consolidated Investment & Contracting Co* v. *Saponaria Shipping Co Ltd; The Virgo* [1978] 3 All ER 988 at p. 994.

'The words "undue hardship" in section 27 should not be construed too narrowly. "Undue hardship" means excessive hardship and where the hardship is due to the fault of the claimant, it means hardship the consequences of which are out of proportion to such fault. *Per* Brandon LJ (as he then was) in *The Aspen Trader* [1981] 1 Lloyd's Rep 273 CA at p. 279. **See also:** *The Pegasus* [1967] 1 Lloyd's Rep 302 CA; *The Jocelyne* [1977] 2 Lloyd's Rep 121.

unilateral discharge - one party's purchase of a release from his obligations under a contract, when the other party has performed his obligations. Compare: **mutual discharge.**

V

valuation - a certification exercise to prevent a dispute from arising. The valuer or expert acts on his own experience and knowledge to determine the reference without necessarily calling any evidence from witnesses. A valuation cannot be questioned and is final. However, the parties must enforce the valuation decision through action in court. Compare: **arbitration.**

valuer - an independent expert who determines the value of a property, the quantity or quality of goods delivered or the amount of compensation to be paid in particular circumstances. However, a valuer is not an arbitrator: 'You cannot make a valuer an arbitraror by calling him so, or vice versa.' *Per* Greer J in *Taylor* v. *Yielding* (1912) 56 SJ at p. 253. A valuer determining a valuation is not an arbitrator or quasi-arbitrator and is liable to an action for negligence: *Palacath Ltd* v. *Flanagan* [1985] 2 All ER 161. Compare : **arbitrator.**

VC - Vice Chancellor. **See: Vice Chancellor.**

Vice Chancellor (VC) - a judge who is the Vice President of the Chancery Division of the High Court of Justice. In practice, his office is by statute to administer and manage the Chancery Division. The Vice Chancellor is also an *ex officio* member of the Court of Appeal.

void - of no legal effect. Null.

void contract- a contract, also known as contract void *ab initio,* which has no legal force from the moment of its conclusion (compare: **voidable contract**) e.g., an illegal contract, a gaming or wagering contract or a contract contravening public policy etc. Contracts that are void but not illegal may be saved by severance.

In relation to an arbitration agreement contained in a void contract, the arbitration agreement falls with the void contract: *Joe Lee Ltd* v. *Lord Dalmeny* [1927] 1 Ch 300. **See also: arbitration** agreement; autonomy of the arbitration clause; doctrine of severability or separability.

voidable contract - a contract which is capable of being set aside of having no legal effect, because of undue influence or mistake or misrepresentation etc. Where a voidable contract is being set aside, it is effected by rescission.

In relation of an arbitration clause, a voidable contract does not annul the arbitration clause contained therein: *Societe Anonyme Hersent v. United Towing Co Ltd and White; The Tradesman* [1961] 2 Lloyd's Rep 183. **See also: arbitration agreement; autonomy of the arbitration clause; doctrine of severability or separability.**

W

waiver - the abandoning or refraining from asserting a legal right. It is now possible under some circumstances to waive one's right of appeal against an arbitral award by entering into an exclusion agreement: See **exclusion agreement.**

A party's appearance and contest in court may operate as a waiver of his right to arbitration since waiver acts by way of estoppel. However, an appearance under protest is not waiver: *Davies* v. *Price* (1865) 34 LJ 8.

Voluntary appearance in the foreign proceedings does not amount to submission to foreign jurisdiction and thus waive the right to arbitration in England: *Tracomin SA*   v. *Sudan Oil Seeds* [1983] 1 All ER 404.

For the purposes of determining whether a judgment given by a court of an overseas country should be recognised or enforced in England and Wales or Northern Ireland, the person against whom the judgment was given shall not be regarded as having submitted to the jurisdiction of the court by reason only of the fact that he appeared (conditionally or otherwise) in proceedings for all or any one or more of the following purposes, namely - (a) to contest the jurisdiction of the court; (b) to ask the court to dismiss or stay the proceedings on the ground that the dispute in question should be submitted to arbitration or to the determination of the courts of another country; (c) to protect or obtain the release of, property seized or threatened with seizure in the proceedings: *Section 33(1) of the Civil Jurisdiction and Judgment Act 1982* (came into operation on 24 August 1982).

'without prejudice' offer - an offer made by one party to the other in an arbitration reference or before the commencement of the arbitration proceedings and is marked 'without prejudice'.

'A "without prejudice" offer can never be referred to by either party at any stage of the proceedings, because it is in the public interest that there should be a procedure whereby the parties can discuss their difference freely and frankly and make offers of settlement without fear of being embarrassed by these exchanges, if, unhappily, they do not lead to a settlement.' *Per* Donaldson J in *Tramountana Armadora SA* v. *Atlantic Shipping Co SA* [1978] 2 All ER 870 at p. 876. **See also: sealed offer; open offer.**

'without prejudice' procedure - a conciliatory exercise usually initiated by one party proposing settlement in a certain manner, the methods of procedure and the number of issues in dispute. The decrease in the number of issues in disputes is often the result of the pre-trial 'without prejudice' discussion prompted by interlocutory procedure of discovery of documents. **See also: conciliation.**

witness - a person who gives evidence in court or in a tribunal. A witness who gives evidence in court must do so on oath or affirmation. A witness in an arbitration reference need not necessarily have to give evidence under oath or affirmation. Moreover, the giving of evidence on oath or affirmation in a commercial arbitration is most unusual. However, the arbitrator, under section 12(2) of the Arbitration Act 1950 has a discretion to examine the witness on oath or affirmation, subject to any express intention of the parties in the arbitration agreement.

words of art - words whose legal interpretation has been fixed so that the legal effect of their use is known, e.g., a paramount clause. **See also: paramount clause.**

World Bank Convention - See: **International Centre for Settlement of Investment Disputes (ICSID).**

World Court - a common term which refers to two international courts set up after the First and Second World war i.e., the Permanent Court of International Justice (PCIJ), established in pursuance of part of the 1919 peace settlement and the International Court of Justice (ICJ), set up in 1945 as the successor to the PCIJ. **See: ICJ.**

Worshipful Company of Arbitrators, the - one of the new livery companies in the City of London, formed nearly ten years ago. There are about 100 livery companies in the City today, the Worshipful

Company of Arbitrators being 93 on the list. It has a total of 236 members (as at December 1984), 155 of whom are Liverymen and the remaining 81 are Freemen. Under its constitution, the total number of Liverymen may not exceed 300. These livery companies exist to provide facilities for fellowship of both social and professional character and the relief of poverty and distress of its members. The Worshipful Company of Arbitrators has recently established a charitable trust, one of its main objects is to promote education with special reference to arbitration.

The various City companies have existed from time immemorial, probably since the first year of the reign of Richard I in 1189.

writ - a court order directing some act of forebearance, especially a writ of summons. **See also: writ of summons.**

writ of execution - a writ used in the enforcement of a judgment. It includes a writ of *fi fa* (see: *fieri facias)*, a writ of delivery, a writ of sequestration, etc. **See also: enforcement of arbitral award; enforcement of judgment.**

writ of summons - also known as a *writ simpliciter*. It commences an action in the High Court, especially one relating to tort (other than trespass to land) or fraud or damages or any case involving contentious issues of facts. An action is brought in the High Court when a writ is issued and not when it is served, But in arbitration, a claimant has to serve a notice on his opponent in order that an arbitration can be deemed to have commenced: *Section 27(3), Arbitration Act 1950.*

Table of Cases

Table of Cases

Table of Cases

Table of Cases

G

H

I

Table of Cases

Table of Cases

Table of Cases

Table of Cases

Table of Cases

Table of Statutes and RSC